Tarot and Love

Enos Long

Tarot
and Love

Enos Long

Tarot and Love

SOJOURNER BOOKS

https://sojournerbooks.com

ISBN: 978-1-7390445-1-0

Table of Contents

Introduction

The Tarot was initially used only as a game; the 78 cards that make it up, whose first copies appeared in northern Italy in the fifteenth century, offered players a range of images taken from the iconography of the time; although the drawings of the cards varied over time, the cards were standardized between the 17th and 18th centuries in the deck we know today as the Tarot of Marseilles.

In the last third of the 18th century, in France, Jean-Baptiste Alliette, under the pseudonym Etteilla, wrote a series of books on the divinatory use of cards. He taught the divinatory use of piquet cards in the *Le petit Etteilla our l'art de tirer les cartes* (Little Etteilla or the art of throwing cards).

Between the years 1783-1785 Etteilla published his work *Manière de se récréer avec le jeu de cartes nommées tarots* (How to amuse oneself with the deck of cards called tarots), in four volumes. With this book, and with the Tarot deck that he published at the end of the 18th century, Etteilla transformed the Tarot into a divinatory tool, leaving behind its origin as a game of cards. In fact, we owe to Etteilla many of the divinatory meanings that we associate with Tarot cards today.

Another important figure in the history of the Tarot is Alphonse Louis Constant, who published his works under the pseudonym Éliphas Lévi, and who was the first to link the Tarot cards (the major arcana) with the Hebrew alphabet in his magnum opus, *Dogme et Rituel de la Haute Magie* (Doctrine and Ritual of High Magic), (1854-56). Throughout the 19th century, other French esotericists dealt with the Tarot, and different card readers, including Marie Anne Adelaide Lenormand, used the Tarot to predict the future of their clients.

Although it was also printed in other parts of Europe, at that time the Tarot was a typically French product, and French esotericists were the first to link it with different hermetic systems. It was not until the end of the 19th century that the Tarot began to interest English esotericists, especially those belonging to the Hermetic Order of the Golden Dawn. This order used the Tarot as a ritual/divinatory tool and its members created their own deck, which was only used by them.

In 1909, a member of the Golden Dawn, which by then had ceased to exist, Arthur Edward Waite, published a Tarot deck that would become the most popular Tarot of our time. That deck is known as the Rider-Waite-Smith (RWS) Tarot, after the names of its publisher (Rider), its creator (Waite), and its illustrator and co-creator (Pamela Colman-Smith). Its major difference with the Tarot of Marseilles is that the Minor Arcana are illustrated with images that make their interpretation easier, also the numeration of two major arcana, Justice and Strength, is inverted.

Since then, the Tarot has spread throughout the world; thousands of different Tarot decks have been published, some based on the Tarot of Marseilles, others following the RWS Tarot, or based on various hermetic systems.

Today many people use the Tarot, not only for divinatory purposes, but also as a tool for the expression of the unconscious and an aid for meditation and decision making.

Also the Tarot can be used to shed light on love and relationships, it can provide information about our tendencies, potentialities and limitations on that field, as well as about the possible types of people who can come into contact with us and their personal traits.

The meanings associated with the Tarot cards shown in this book can be applied to the Tarot of Marseilles and the Rider-Waite-Smith (RWS) Tarot, as well as to most Tarot decks whose card layouts follow the Tarot of Marseilles pattern.

The cards shown in this book are from a traditional Tarot of Marseilles from the early 18th century, which we have faithfully reproduced, without any retouching, to preserve the original character of the old-fashioned printed Tarot decks[1].

---

1   The first Tarot decks, created in northern Italy in the 15th century, were exquisite art works, hand-painted by artists for aristocratic patrons. Only when Tarot decks began to be printed with wooden molds (xylography), which lowered their cost, did they become popular. At that time (17th, 18th and part of the 19th centuries) after being printed by xylographic methods, the Tarot decks were colored by placing different stencils on them, one for each color, which allowed the cards to be painted by hand quickly. Cards produced this way showed numerous blemishes, such as smudges and poorly printed areas, making them unique, no two decks were exactly alike.

How to Understand Tarot Readings

This book shows the meanings of the Tarot cards, both general and directly related to love. However, it is important to understand that the cards should not be interpreted as isolated elements, but as parts of a whole. That whole is the arrangement of cards in the Tarot reading.

When we throw the cards, they are distributed in different ways, depending on the spread we use. There are many different types of Tarot spreads, each with their own purpose and style. Here we present some of the most common Tarot spreads:

Spread of three cards: This is one of the simplest spreads of Tarot. It consists of drawing three cards, which represent the past, the present and the future. This spread is useful to obtain an overview of a specific situation or problem, and it is the one that we will use to exemplify how to interpret Tarot cards (although we do not assign the past, present and future to the different cards).

Celtic Cross Spread: This is a more complex spread that uses 10 cards to provide a more detailed reading. This spread includes cards that represent the past, present, future, obstacles, external influences, fears, hopes, and the final result.

The Thot or Golden Dawn Spread: Although often it is called the Golden Dawn spread, this spread originally appeared in the little white book that accompanies the Thot Tarot. It uses 15 cards, divided into five trios, representing the current situation, what can be changed, what cannot be changed (karma), and two different futures, either related or alternate. This spread uses the elemental dignities system, rather than inverted cards, to determine the status of each card.

Astrological Wheel Spread: This spread uses 12 cards, each representing a zodiac sign and an astrological house. This spread is ideal for gaining a deeper understanding of the cosmic energies that influence our lives.

These are just a few of the many Tarot spreads out there. Each of them can be useful in different situations and for different purposes, so it is important to choose the right spread for our specific situation, or simply the one we like best.

Actually, the most important thing is not which spread we choose, but how we interpret all the cards in a reading as a whole. The cards are not isolated entities, but each of them influence their neighbors, and the pattern formed by all the cards laid on table tells a story that we have to weave together. If we are not capable of doing that, we will only see a series of isolated meanings, which can often even be contradictory, and which will not clarify much the situation represented by the Tarot reading.

We can think of Tarot readings as plays, with different characters (the court cards: Page, Knight, Queen and King) and with multiple tendencies, some positive and others harmful. The Major Arcana (cards I-XXI and the Fool, which in the Tarot of Marseilles is unnumbered and in other decks has the number 0) indicate the main forces in play and the ten numbered cards of the four suits: Wands, Cups, Swords and Coins or Pentacles provide more details.

Possibly the most practical way to learn to interpret Tarot readings is by seeing specific examples. All the examples that follow are simple and consist of trios, that is, groups of three cards, because that is the easiest way to understand how the cards interact with each other; if we used more cards, it would unnecessarily complicate our interpretation of the reading; but to take our first steps in the Tarot we must concentrate on the essentials.

By arranging the cards in horizontal trios, the central card is always the most significant, it points to the core of the situation. Inverted cards are indicated by the word inv., next to the card name.

Let's look at some examples, which will clarify this topic.

FIRST EXAMPLE

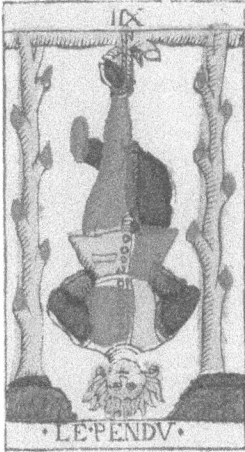

XII The Hanged Man	Page of Cups	5 of Coins
Indecision, suspension of all action	Proposal, beginning of a relationship	Indigence, deprivation; lovers

Interpretation: The Page of Cups, which is located in the center of this reading, and for this reason is the most important card, symbolizes a young, sensitive and kind person, who wants to enter our life, help us and make us a proposal, although it can also indicate the birth of a feeling in ourselves. This card is an appeal to love. If we are already in a relationship with someone, the Page of Cups can indicate a marriage proposal or at least a bid to take the relationship to the next level.

On the other hand, the card located on the left, The Hanged Man indicates that we are focused inwardly, trying to decide what to do, perhaps reluctant to take risks in love affairs. This is not a tenable position in the long term, we are exposed, our unwillingness to become romantically involved is public knowledge. But since The Hanged Man indicates extreme introspection, we will not be the ones to take the first step, but the Page of Cups will knock on our doors.

If we are already in a relationship, The Hanged Man suggests that we are excessively focused on ourselves, in this case the Page of Cups is a wake-up call for us to pay more attention to our partner and open our hearts.

The third card, which completes this spread, is the Five of Coins, which is a card that has two aspects, on the one hand it indicates economic hardship and indigence, and on the other, good luck in love. Having the Page of Cups in the center, it is clear that in this reading, the Five of Coins means good luck in love, lovers. This card can indicate either a new relationship, or the revival of a relationship that we had neglected, as the The Hanged Man seems to indicate.

SECOND EXAMPLE

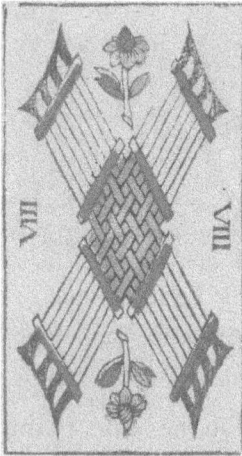

8 of Wands	XIX The Sun	6 of Cups (inv.)
High hopes, things that happen quickly	Success, marital happiness	Reluctance to change, bad influences

Interpretation: The central card, The Sun, is one of the most positive major arcana, it promises us happiness and mental clarity that will allow us to discard all doubt, and achieve what we long for. It is also a card of love and brotherhood, conducive to all social relationships, including love ones.

If we are already in a relationship, The Sun suggests an expansive and happy phase, with excellent communication. This card reflects a flourishing couple relationship, with a great amount of energy and vitality, which allows us to enjoy the intimacy, passion and harmony of our relationship. If we have a conflict with our partner, we can solve it.

The card on the left, the Eight of Wands, suggests that we are full of energy, very encouraged by a new love or by plans that we want to carry out. Things rush and we may make hasty decisions or travel, since this card also means travel or love messages. Since it is next to The Sun, we can conclude that any relationship we have or want to establish will develop quickly, because our understanding and communication with our partner (current or future) is fluid and clear.

The third card, the inverted Six of Cups, is not propitious, although it is not too bad either. It suggests that sometimes we limit ourselves, that we don't look forward and we resist change. It also indicates bad influences, friendships of little value that harm us, or perhaps bad habits that we drag from the past. This card introduces delays, but in no way can counteract the strength of The Sun, at worse it can tarnish and delay our happiness a little. But this card teaches us that if we want to fully enjoy the present, we must leave behind the bad habits and toxic relationships of the past.

THIRD EXAMPLE

Two of Swords (inv.)	6 of Swords	Ace of Coins
Conflict, betrayal	Overcoming difficulties	Happiness and well-being

Interpretation: As we can see, swords predominate in this reading, which usually are not considered good for love, since them are primarily related to intellect and conflict. But despite that, swords can very well describe many human relationships and certain periods of our lives. In this case, we have the Six of Swords in the center, a card that indicates progress, overcoming difficulties and change of scenery. This card also tells us that we must broaden our horizons and evolve spiritually in order to overcome the interpersonal conflicts that affect us. The teaching of the Six of Swords is that we can and should leave toxic relationships behind, and to achieve this the best way is to grow spiritually, to stay out of the reach of people who harm us. For this reason this card is related

to travel by water; such journey suggests estrangement and also marks a clear boundary between the two shorelines separated by water.

On the left we have the Two of Swords; inverted, as presented here, this card indicates discord, lack of control, betrayal, lies, disloyalty and false friends. For this reason, we mentioned toxic relationships in the previous paragraph; this reading tells us that we must separate ourselves from and abandon those who harm us. If we are already in a relationship, these two cards that we have mentioned suggest a separation, although it is not possible to say if it will be permanent or temporary. The reversed Two of Swords also tells us that we must balance our life, which is out of control, and sometimes it is necessary to distance ourselves in order to see things in perspective and recover our emotional balance.

The third card, the Ace of Coins is very positive. All aces promise new beginnings, and the Ace of Coins indicates a period of security, contentment, and abundance. In the realm of love, and relating this card to the previous two, we see the result of spiritual growth, obtained by following a new path, which leads us from conflict (Two of Swords) to happiness and peace (Ace of Coins). Of course, the Ace of Coins also implies material abundance, something that will help us stabilize our new life.

FOURTH EXAMPLE

XVII The Star	5 of Cups	8 of Cups
Insight, inspiration, hope	Disappointment, regret, loss	Wandering, abandoned relationship

Interpretation: The central card, the Five of Cups is associated with disappointment, loss and sorrow. In love, it can indicate mourning for the loss of a person, regret for the mistakes made that led us to lose someone, or disappointment with someone with whom we were or are intimately linked. Being the central card, these meanings indicate our current or future situation, now let's see how the neighboring cards describe the evolution of this situation.

The Star indicates clarity of vision and inspiration, which are the qualities required to get out of the depression that the Five of Cups symbolizes. What we need to cope with our loss or disappointment is more mental clarity, if we open our eyes we will see that there are possibilities that we did not imagine, but as long as we continue with our eyes fixed on the earth, regretting what we have lost, we will not be able to see the path that will take us out of the emotional quagmire in which we find ourselves. That is why it is said that The Star promises us help, that we will receive when we least expect it, but we can only take advantage of that help if we have our eyes open.

The third card, the Eight of Cups, completes our interpretation. This card indicates that we are recovering from a love disappointment and our situation is unstable. We still haven't decided what we want to do with our life and we are looking for new options. It is said that this is the pilgrim's card, because it indicates a search for meaning, for higher values to guide our life. We can see that this card tells us what we must do in order to receive the inspiration that The Star promises. If our current relationship only brings us bitterness, or if we don't know how to overcome our problems, this card encourages us to leave behind the feelings or people that make us suffer and to find a new path. The fact that The Star is also part of this reading gives us hope that we will be able to follow a better path in our life and recover our lost happiness.

From all that we have said, it is clear that this reading does not promise us immediate happiness or quick solutions to our problems, but simply shows us how to overcome a bad situation. Likewise, we must not forget that The Star is the card of hope, and it promises us that someone will reach out to us to help us overcome our sadness.

FIFTH EXAMPLE

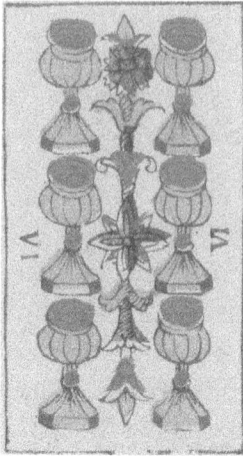

6 of Cups	VI The Lovers	Queen of Cups (inv.)
Nostalgia, influences from the past	Good choice, union, marriage	Beguiling and vicious woman

Interpretation: The VI° arcane, in the central position, The Lovers, means good choice, union, marriage. This card, in the Marseille Tarot, shows a man between two women, who are apparently fighting over him (the RWS Tarot only shows a couple, that is, it shows the final consequence, not the previous choice). The usual meaning is that the lover must choose well (the original title of this card in French is *L'Amoureux*, that is to say "the lover"), following his heart. This card tells us that we must harmonize our feelings with the outside world.

The two neighboring cards help us to understand the influences that affect the "lover" (which may be the querent).

The Six of Cups is related to nostalgia and memories of the past. As for love, this card can indicate that we are remembering an old love or that a friendship or love from the past reappears in our lives. This card suggests positive influences from the past, happiness or love that comes from the past. These influences can be internal (nostalgia, memories of the past) and/or external (such as an old love or friendship that returns to our life).

On the other hand, the card on the right, the Queen of Cups, is inverted, it indicates a woman who wants to manipulate us for her own amusement, without caring about our well-being; but from a psychological point of view, this card also suggests that we are insecure and do not know how to express our emotions, which makes us act with hostility and withdraw into ourselves.

In summary, here we have several possible interpretations for this reading:

The Six of Cups is someone who comes back from our past, and the Queen of Cups (inv.) is a seductive and vicious woman who is trying to manipulate us. The choice is not difficult, on the one hand we have happiness and a lasting union, and on the other a mirage, which can be pleasant, but it will not last, or, if it lasts, it can turn into a nightmare, because the Queen of Cups inverted does not bode well, while the Six of Cups indicates good influences.

On the other hand, if we see the reading from a rather psychological point of view, on the one hand we have nostalgia, memories of the past, and on the other distrust, reluctance to express our feelings (the Queen of Cups inverted). In the center, The Lovers indicate a great attraction towards a certain person, but our mistrust does not allow us to express our feelings, we prefer to delight in the memories of our past rather than take action in the present. In this case, the interpretation would be that we have a very good opportunity to become emotionally attached to someone (including marriage), but our doubts and longings will delay or prevent that.

We could also see the Six of Cups as a person who comes from the past, and the Queen of Cups (inv.) as a symbol that represents our doubts and fears, which make us reject those who approach us.

In short, someone from our past will return to our lives, perhaps other people will interfere, or may be our doubts will hinder us, but we should not waste this opportunity.

SIXTH EXAMPLE

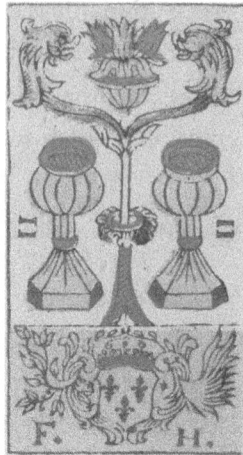

8 of Swords (inv.)	2 of Coins	4 of Swords
Liberation	Uncertainty, ups and downs	Withdrawal, loneliness

Interpretation: The central card, the Two of Coins points to an ambivalent attitude or relationship. It may mean a relationship with a person who is unstable, oscillating between warmth and contempt, disturbing and confusing us a lot. Of course, we may not be fully decided neither and we don't know if we should try to take the relationship to the next level or, instead, discard it.

Fortunately the Eight of Swords (inv.) indicates that things will finally become clear, we will overcome the confusion that surrounds us — and the manipulations of other people — and we will see things clearly. When we recover our freedom of thought and action, we will be able to left behind the indecision that bogs us down.

The third card, the Four of Swords, shows us how to carry out what the Eight of Swords (inv.) promises us. This card indicates a time of withdrawal and solitude, when we temporarily withdraw from our relationships and try to calm down, meditating and seeing things from a new perspective.

In short, in order to see things more clearly we need to calm down, and take a little distance from a complicated relationship. Nothing in this reading promises a sustainable relationship, rather the opposite. Possibly taking distance and freeing ourselves is the best option.

Of course, an alternative interpretation could be that we are going through an unclear and uncertain period in our life, in which case the reading would not refer to a problematic relationship in particular, but to a period during which we cannot achieve much in the field of love, because we lack clarity and focus.

Let us bear in mind that both interpretations are not exclusive, since they can be complementary.

SEVENTH EXAMPLE

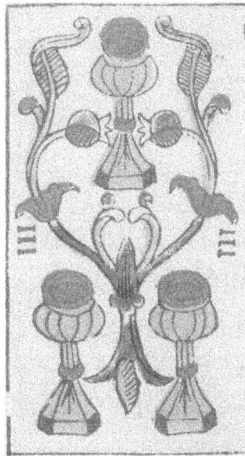

XIV Temperance	3 of Cups	XV The Devil
Harmony, tolerance	Abundance, enjoyment of life	Bad relationship, force majeure

Interpretation: The central card, the Three of Cups represents abundance, celebration, friendship and emotional connection with our friends and loved ones. In love, this card can signify a happy and satisfying relationship where the partners feel emotionally connected. It can indicate a happy celebration or event in the family, such as an engagement, an anniversary, or even a wedding.

What makes the interpretation of this reading difficult — at least at first glance — are the two major arcana that flank the Three of Cups. Let's see how we can reconcile them.

Temperance primarily indicates moderation; on a material level, and trying to relate this card to the celebration that the Three of Cups suggests, it would indicate abstention or moderate consumption of alcohol, or frugality in eating. Regarding interpersonal relationships, this card indicates harmony, tolerance and a very good relations with other people, and it can even mean marriage.

So far everything is positive, the two cards we have seen paint us a picture of harmony and happiness in a family or a group of friends; the third card, The Devil, however complicates the picture.

The Devil, indicates bad influences (both from people, and from obsessions that we may have, drugs or alcohol). But on the other hand, it is also related to irresistible influences, which in the Tarot are called force majeure, that is, an unpredictable and unavoidable circumstance that prevents us from doing something or that forces us to follow a certain course of action, and that "force" it is not necessarily evil, just irresistible. That is to say that The Devil can also indicate the force of destiny, something that we cannot control. That "something" can be a passion that arises within us or an external influence.

Let's look at several possible interpretations:

We can consider the two major arcana that flank the Three of Cups as the two poles of a situation: one of harmony and the other of excesses. From this point of view, this reading may indicate a relationship based on enjoying the good things in life (central card), but which oscillates from harmony (tolerance and moderation) to excess (selfishness and extreme lack of control). It is hardly necessary to say that this type of relationship can be very exhausting and does not seem to be sustainable in the long term.

We can also see the three cards in a temporal progression. Initially we started from a harmonious and happy relationship (Temperance and Three of Cups), but at one point a new influence enters that changes everything and we don't know where it will lead us, it is The Devil in the sense of "force majeure." It can be a passion that drags us or a person who opens the door to a new world, frightening, but irresistible. Paraphrasing J. L. Borges (albeit with a small modification): "The path is like an arrow, deadly straight, but in the cracks is the Devil, who lies in wait." The end result is unpredictable, unless other cards make it clearer.

EIGHTH EXAMPLE

Knight of Cups

Proposal, opportunity

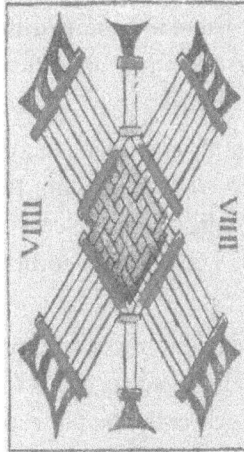

9 of Wands

Pause in the fight

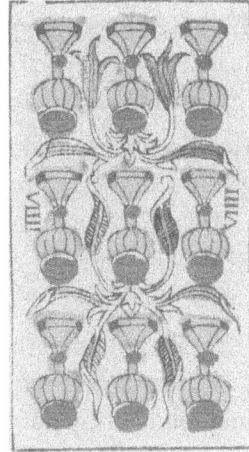

9 of Coins (inv.)

Deception, robbery

Interpretation: The central card, the Nine of Wands, indicates perseverance and resistance, suggesting that we have gone through a troubled period in our relationships, but that we are prepared to overcome any obstacle that arises in our love life and social relationships, because we know what we want. It also promises us that everything will end well.

The Nine of Coins, which flanks the central card, is inverted, which clarifies the nature of the problems pointed to by the Nine of Wands. We suffered some disappointment, someone deceived us, and the break in this relationship, which was not easy, but rather bitter and conflictive, affected us deeply.

The third card, the Knight of Cups, throws a ray of light into the somewhat bleak picture of this reading. In human relationships, the Knight of Cups indicates a romantic approach, in which love and passion are the main engines. This card suggests the appearance of a sensitive, creative, affectionate and passionate man, who can be a great sentimental partner. The Knight of Cups also invites us to connect with our deepest feelings and let intuition and heart guide us towards love.

However, the Nine of Wands tells us that the newcomer's positive influence will gradually make itself felt, it will still take us a while until we overcome past disappointment.

In summary, after suffering a disappointment in love we will have a new opportunity, do not let it pass

A Tarot Spread Dedicated Entirely to Love

We have already seen that there are many different Tarot spreads. If we search the Internet or browse through different Tarot books, we can find a wide variety in this regard.

Here we offer a relatively simple spread, focused on love. Although we group the cards into three trios, following the pattern of the Thot or Golden Dawn spread, we will not use elemental dignities (which only work with upright cards), but we will combine upright and inverted cards.

We'll leave it up to the reader to choose the method they prefer to shuffle the cards (as long as it allows some cards to be inverted). The easiest method is to lay out the cards over the table and, spreading your hands over the cards, shuffle them in such a way that they rotate and combine randomly.

After shuffling, the cards will be arranged on the table following this scheme:

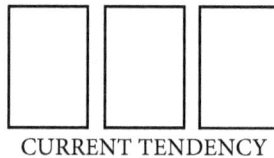

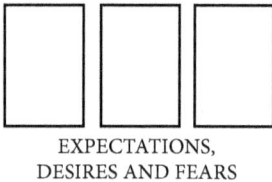

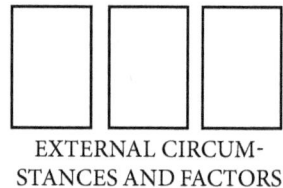

CURRENT TENDENCY

EXPECTATIONS,
DESIRES AND FEARS

EXTERNAL CIRCUM-
STANCES AND FACTORS

When we compare a card with the neighboring cards (to determine which meanings we will apply), we will do it within each of the trios, which we will analyze as if they were independent entities, to simplify the interpretative process.

As we can see in the upper figure, in this spread, the upper trio indicates the current trend, where are we going, which is something we can modify with our actions, and which simply suggests what may happen in the future.

The lower left trio indicates our expectations, desires and fears, that is, the emotional and spiritual aspect of our social relationships. It may also show people or events from our past, that still influence us.

The lower right trio refers to external circumstances and factors and the purely objective aspect of our love/social relationships, here can appear our friends and relatives, who are close to our hearts, but also our enemies.

The next two pages show an example of this spread.

EXAMPLE OF A TAROT CARD READING ORIENTED TO LOVE

King of Cups

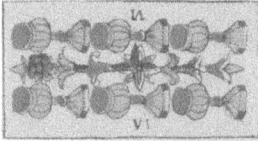

6 of Cups

XVI The Tower (inv.)

10 of Coins

4 of Wands

King of Coins

8 of Swords

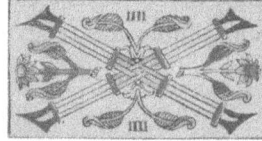

XII The Hanged Man (inv.)

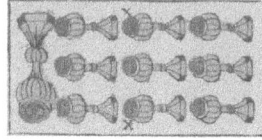

XIX The Sun

We will start with the lower left trio, which indicates our expectations, desires and fears. In the center we see The Hanged Man, inverted, which indicates a tendency to leave everything for tomorrow, indulging in illusions, gratifying in the short term but of no use at the end; in fact them only increase our isolation. In other words, our emotional life is stagnant.

The Eight of Swords, that appears on one side, explains why we are stuck. This card suggests that we are paralyzed because we do not see things clearly, possibly we are trapped in an unsatisfactory relationship, although it is also possible that we deceive ourselves, refusing to recognize reality, which would force us to do something concrete to solve our problems.

The third card in this trio is very positive. The Sun, dispels darkness and allows us to see things clearly. This card indicates healing, which tells us that we can res tore our mental clarity and joy in life, but only if we face reality honestly and remove our blindfolds.

Moving on to the lower right trio, which refers to external factors, the central card, the Four of Wands, like all four, indicates stability. Other meanings are peace, harmony, marriage and partnership.

To its left we see the Ten of Coins, which clarifies the previous card a lot. The Ten of Coins is a card related to the family in the broad sense, that is, more than the nuclear family, the extended family. This card promises material security, dominions and an increase in wealth. By combining the meanings of these two cards it is clear that we enjoy material stability and that we are not alone, but that our family supports us, that we have a solid foundation — at least from the material point of view — in life.

The third card, the King of Coins can point to a person, perhaps the head of the family, someone steady, capable, trustworthy and experienced, who supports us. It can also indicate the qualities we have, which reinforces the message of this trio: we have a solid foundation and we are not alone, even if we do not feel that way emotionally (as the lower left trio indicates).

Finally, the upper central trio has the Six of Cups in the center, which is related to nostalgia and memories of the past. As for love, this card can indicate that we are remembering an old love or that a friendship or love from the past reappears in our lives.

Unfortunately, to his right appears The Tower, inverted, which indicates an unsatisfactory relationship, which we cannot improve or abandon. It can also suggest some inability to share our feelings and to communicate with others. These meanings remind us of the message of the cards of the lower left trio; now, while the cards of the lower left trio point to our psychological situation, here we see, in The Tower (inv.) the external concomitant of those feelings, a toxic relationship that imprisons us like a prison.

On the other side of the Six of Cups, we have the King of Cups, who extends his cup offering a way out of this bad situation, and promising healing of our love sorrows. The King of Cups is associated with emotional maturity, deep and sincere feelings, and is often associated with a therapist or psychologist. Taken to the field of love, this card can indicate a stable relationship, full of affection and emotional commitment, and as it is flanking the Six of Cups, it would be someone we already met in the past. This card is also associated with understanding and empathy, suggesting that in a fruitful relationship, both parties can communicate effectively and understand each other's needs.

To conclude with the interpretation of this reading, we can analyze it in two different ways, one focused on external factors (such as a toxic relationship) and another more psychological, which points to our own shortcomings, although of course we can also combine both interpretations.

The "external" interpretation would be that we are trapped in a toxic relationship, but our family offers us their support and we have the material means to free ourselves when we choose to do so. We may need help to get ahead and leave toxic dependencies behind, but the King of Cups not only symbolizes someone who helps us, but also indicates the path to follow to have a fuller emotional life, that is, to achieve emotional maturity.

Seeing this reading from a more psychological point of view, it tells us that we are trapped as well, but because of our fears and prejudices, which prevent us from seeing reality clearly and force us to repeat over and over our old patterns of behavior that do not allow us to be free or happy. Here, the King of Cups could be a psychologist, or a benevolent father figure, who helps us clarify ourselves and have a more fulfilling life. The King of Cups is associated with intuition and emotional intelligence, and these are the qualities that we must cultivate in ourselves.

In both cases, we will need help to overcome our problems, emotionally we have the support of the King of Cups, and in the material side, the help of our family.

Practical Application

The examples we have seen give us a practical idea of how the "theme" of a reading can be put together. We encourage our readers to try not only the comprehensive love spread that we have described, but also different ones, until they find their favorite one.

Many times it is difficult to choose which of the meanings associated with a card should be emphasized, and as we have seen, that can only be done by using the neighboring cards, because the cards influence each other. The examples presented previously, in the form of different trios of cards, explain this process in a practical way.

We believe that grouping the cards in trios is the best way to understand how the cards interact with each other; if we used more cards we would unnecessarily complicate our interpretation. When using three cards, we can often apply the dialectical method, which consists of thesis (central card), antithesis and synthesis, which makes it easier to analyze the interaction of the cards, other times the cards will boost each other.

At first, getting the "theme of the reading" seems to be a very difficult thing, we only see a group of cards, each one with its own meanings, which are sometimes difficult to integrate into a coherent whole, so it is important to emphasize the importance of practice to be able to interpret Tarot readings fluently. Practice is necessary not only to memorize the meanings of the cards, which is the first step, but also, to be able to interpret the readings as a whole, relating the cards to each other in such a way that we see the general theme.

Another detail that is often overlooked by the tarot reader who is just starting out in the art of reading cards, is that Tarot cards, in a way, are like people, they have virtues and defects. Usually the flaws are associated with the card in the inverted position (especially in court cards), but when we apply any Tarot card to a person, in the real world, we must take into account the full range of meanings of the card, both good and bad, as a description of that person, or their behavior, their strengths and weaknesses. Of course, depending on the position of the card (upright or inverted), the person the card describes will act in one way or another, that is to say, either their virtues or defects will predomi-nate. But we must always take into account the total sum of meanings of the card, in order to understand in depth the person or situation it describes.

If we persevere in the study of the Tarot and in the practice of its read-ings, little by little we will be able to draw clear conclusions from the cards in an intuitive way, but for this intuition to be valid, in the first place we must be completely familiar with their meanings and with the divinatory process, that is why it is so important to do as many read-ings as possible, even if we don't ask anything in particular; they will be "training" readings, not being related to any person or situation of the real world. But nevertheless, they won't stop showing us glimpses of ourselves!

Major Arcana

0. The Fool[1]

DIVINATORY MEANING
Spontaneity, boldness, extravagance. Negligence, little reflection, fickleness, indiscretion. Insecurity, voluntary abandonment of material goods. Beginning of an adventure or a journey. Freedom from conventions and norms. Keep options open. Give up control. Pay attention to the here and now. Message: keep moving.

INVERTED
Lack of common sense, passion, obsession, madness, foolishness, impulsiveness, influenceability. Restlessness, lack of purpose, poor planning skills. Hindered trip. It can also indicate lymphatism, swelling and abscesses.

The Fool is a card that is often interpreted as representing freedom, spontaneity, change, and adventure. In the context of love, this card can mean that we are looking to experience new emotions and sensations in our romantic relationships, and we are willing to risk everything in our search for love.

The Fool suggests that this is a good time to seek new experiences in love and be adventurous in our relationships. It may be the ideal occasion to explore new activities, places and people that allow us to expand our emotional horizons and discover new aspects of ourselves.

On the other hand, if we are in a relationship, The Fool may indicate that we need to break the routine and monotony of our love life. Maybe it's time to do something exciting and different with our partner, like traveling together to an unknown place or trying new activities that lead us to experience new and exciting sensations.

Overall, The Fool is a card that reminds us that love can be an exciting adventure and that spontaneity and freedom are important to keep passion and romance alive.

When this card is inverted it indicates obsessions, frantic passion, lack of judgment and influenceability, so we could become toys, both of our own passions and of other people. It also suggests that we are stuck emotionally or in a relationship, and cannot move forward.

---

1   Unnumbered card in the Tarot of Marseilles.

·LE ·MAT ·

I. The Magician

DIVINATORY MEANING
Originality. Initiative, center of action, firm and well-directed will, start of a venture with the available tools, spontaneous intelligence. Self-possession, autonomy, emancipation from all prejudice. Eloquence, dexterity, skill, finesse, business acumen. Lawyer, orator, diplomat. Physical power over (the own) illnesses of a mental or nervous nature.

INVERTED
Weak willed, inexperienced, incapable, someone who doesn't know what he's doing. An illusionist, schemer, careerist, politician, charlatan, impostor, liar, thief, exploiter of the naive. Diseases of the nervous system.

The Magician is a card that is often interpreted as representing creative power, the will to manifest our desires, and the ability to influence others. In the context of love, this card can indicate that we have the capacity to take control of our love life and enter into meaningful and fulfilling relationships.

If we don't have a partner, The Magician can indicate that this is a good time to work on ourselves and our social skills to attract someone special. This card reminds us that we have everything we need to have a happy and fulfilling love relationship, and that we must trust our abilities and our intuition to find the right path to love. Let's note that The Magician appears in front of an outdoor table, showing everyone his abilities, in the same way, if we want to find new relationships, we must open up to the world and be active participants in the social scene.

On the other hand, if we are already in a relationship, The Magician can indicate that we have the ability to influence our partner in a positive and constructive way. We may need to work on our ability to communicate clearly, listen actively, and express our feelings effectively in order to achieve a more fulfilling and lasting relationship.

In general, The Magician is a card that reminds us that we are able to create our own love reality, and that we must trust our abilities and our intuition to take control of our love life and build meaningful and lasting relationships.

·LE·PATELEVR·

If it is inverted, The Magician indicates that either we are not up to what it takes to establish a meaningful relationship, or we abuse our relationships with insincerity and lies, creating false illusions. If the reading suggests that this card represents another person, we must beware of lies and disloyalty.

II. The High Priestess / The Popess

DIVINATORY MEANING
The gate of the sanctuary. Wisdom, silence, patience, discretion (this card shares these virtues with the IXth major arcana, The Hermit), reserve, meditation, modesty, resignation and piety. Respect for sacred things. Hidden influences (in art and spirit), mystery, intuition. Know how to set limits. Teacher. Well-considered decision.

INVERTED
Emotional block. Dissimulation, hidden intentions, rancor, laziness, intolerance, fanaticism. It becomes heavy and passive, it is like a burden. Delay, tension and clumsiness in relationships. Ill-considered decision.

The High Priestess is a card that is often interpreted as representing intuition, inner wisdom, and a connection to the spiritual world. In the context of love, this card can indicate that we need to listen to our intuition and put our actions in sync with our deepest desires, to find answers in our love life.

If we are alone, The High Priestess can indicate that we need to take some time to connect with our inner being and explore our true desires in love. Perhaps we need to be more selective with our romantic choices and be more attentive to the intuitive signals that indicate the right person for us.

On the other hand, if we already have a partner, The High Priestess can indicate that we need to trust our intuition and listen to our inner feelings to solve any problem in our relationship. We may need to be more aware of our needs and desires and effectively communicate them to our partner to strengthen our emotional and spiritual connection.

In general, The High Priestess is a card that reminds us that we need to trust our intuition and connect with our inner wisdom to find answers in our love life. It tells us that sometimes the answers we seek are not found in the outside world, but in our own inner being.

When it is inverted, this card indicates emotional blockage, obstacles and dissimulation. If we have an established relationship, it may be stagnant and we are unable to communicate effectively with our partner. If we are alone, it may be because we are too focused on ourselves. If we

want to establish new social relationships (let's focus on that step, without rushing to achieve more intimate relationships) perhaps we should be more flexible and tolerant with others and try to express our feelings better. Let's offer others the same breadth of judgment and acceptance that we expect them to give us. Instead waiting for the other to take the first step, let's open our hearts, reach out to others without expecting anything in return.

III. The Empress

DIVINATORY MEANING
Good judgment, intelligence, education, civilizing influence. Charm, courtesy, affability, elegance. Abundance, wealth. Marriage, fertility, sweetness. Improvement and renewal of the situation. Continuous action power.

INVERTED
Affection, pose, frivolity, coquetry, vanity. Disdain, presumption. Unnecessary luxury. Sensitive to flattery. Lack of refinement. Discussions at all levels. Hesitation, lack of concentration. Sterility.

The Empress is a card that is often interpreted as representing femininity, fertility, and abundance. In the context of love, this card can indicate that we are in a moment of emotional fulfillment and we are ready to receive love and affection in our lives. It may also indicate marriage.

If we are alone, The Empress can indicate that this is a good time to work on our self-esteem and our ability to love ourselves. The card reminds us that we have the necessary qualities, and that we must trust our skills and our courtesy and elegance to attract someone special. It can also be a good time to explore our creative interests and express our femininity and sensuality in order to attract someone who values these qualities. On the other hand, The Empress can also refer to a person with the characteristics of this card — charm, courtesy, good judgment, etc. — who enters our life.

On the other hand, if we are already in a relationship, The Empress can indicate that we are enjoying a moment of harmony and emotional balance with our partner. It can be a good time to strengthen the emotional and physical connection with our partner, and to work on joint creative projects that allow us to express our love and creativity.

In general, The Empress is a card that reminds us of the importance of valuing ourselves and cultivating healthy and balanced love relationships. She teaches us that in order to receive love and caring in our lives, we must first learn to love ourselves and to express ourselves courteously and gracefully, in a genuine and authentic way.

When this card appears inverted, it is a call to work on our empathy and to try to connect with others, sincerely and discarding appearanc-

es. Let's avoid discussions and conflicts; instead pretending that others serve us, we should rather think what we can do for them.

IV. The Emperor

DIVINATORY MEANING
Power, leadership, authority, firmness, rigor, accuracy, fairness and positivism. Realization. Powerful protector. Balanced intelligence that does not exceed the utilitarian terrain.

INVERTED
Stubbornness, lack of idealism, obstinate adversary, megalomania, abuse of authority. Inconsistency, weak will. Loss of control, instability. Fall, loss of material assets.

The Emperor is a card that is represents power, authority, stability, and protection. In the context of love, this card can indicate that we tend to structure our love life well in order to feel safe and protected.

If we are alone, The Emperor can indicate that we need to set clear boundaries in our relationships and be selective with our romantic choices. The card reminds us that we are a person with a lot of power and authority, and that we must use this energy to attract someone who lives up to our expectations and who respects our boundaries and values.

On the other hand, if we are in a relationship, The Emperor can indicate that we need to establish clear limits with our partner and be more firm in our decisions and actions. It may be a good time to work on communication and conflict resolution effectively, to create a stable and lasting relationship.

In general, The Emperor is a card that reminds us of the importance of establishing clear boundaries and solid structures in our love relationships. It emphasizes that in order to create a healthy and lasting relationship, we need to have power and authority over our own lives and be selective with our romantic choices.

If it is inverted, The Emperor indicates that we may be abusing other people, being excessively controlling and despotic. Emotionally, it indicates immaturity, insecurity, which we mask by abusing others. If we continue down that path and do not learn to be more flexible and tolerant, we will end up alone.

V. The Hierophant / The Pope

DIVINATORY MEANING
Loyalty, organization, respectability. Moral guidance, teaching, generosity and indulgence, meekness. It is not a strong card but it offers support. Initiation, change of mentality. Religious or scientific vocation. Doctor, psychologist; consult with a specialist.

INVERTED
Close adherence to outdated conventions and norms, an inflexible character, unable to adapt, out of touch with reality. Immorality, hypocrisy. Bureaucrat, judgmental boss, narrow-minded moralist, authoritarian professor, limited theorist, counselor devoid of practical sense. Lack of spiritual support.

The Hierophant is a card that is often interpreted as representing spirituality, morality, and religious wisdom. In the context of love, this card can indicate that we are searching for a deeper emotional and spiritual connection in our love life.

If we are alone, The Hierophant can indicate that we need to seek a deeper emotional and spiritual connection in our love relationships. The card reminds us that in order to find a meaningful and lasting relationship, we need to find someone who shares our values and spirituality. It can also be a good time to explore our spiritual beliefs and our connection to the divine in order to attract someone who is on the same page as us.

On the other hand, if we are in a relationship, The Hierophant can indicate that this is a good time to work on communication and emotional and spiritual connection with our partner. It is conducive to exploring shared spiritual beliefs and values together, and finding a deeper connection through prayer, meditation, or other spiritual practices. If we are not married, this may be a good time to get married.

Overall, The Hierophant is a card that reminds us of the importance of seeking a deeper emotional and spiritual connection in our love relationships. It reminds us that in order to find a meaningful and lasting relationship, we need to be in tune with our values and spirituality, and look for someone who shares our world-view and connection to the divine.

·LE·PAPE·

When it is inverted, it indicates hypocrisy, narrow-mindedness, that we are following outdated standards of behavior and it is very difficult for us to adapt to others. We prefer to hide behind a mask of civility rather than express our true feelings, that we repress.

VI. The Lovers

DIVINATORY MEANING
Choice or decision, examination, longing. Fight between sacred and profane love. Marriage, love, union of opposites, attraction, balance, openness to inspiration. Tests passed. Harmony of the inner life and the outside world. Follow your heart.

INVERTED
Disorder, failure, divorce, unhappy love and setbacks of all kinds. Frustrated marriage, dangerous temptation. Danger of being seduced. Misconduct, debauchery and weakness. Fights, infidelity. Emotional instability. A love triangle that generates tensions (it can be between mother and partner).

The Lovers tells us that we are at a point in our lives in which we must choose which path we should take. In the context of love, this card indicates that we are faced with an important decision in our love life, and that we must choose between two mutually exclusive options. The Lovers, in the Marseille Tarot, shows a man between two women, who are apparently fighting over him (the RWS Tarot only shows a couple, that is, it shows the final consequence, not the previous choice).

If we are alone, The Lovers may indicate that we cannot put off making an important decision regarding our love life any longer. It may be that we find ourselves between two options, such as choosing between two people we like or deciding between continuing on our own or committing to a serious relationship. The card reminds us that we must make a conscious and mature decision, and that we need to seriously weigh the consequences of our decisions. This card also may mean marriage, if other cards confirm that interpretation.

On the other hand, if we are in a relationship, The Lovers can indicate that it is a good time to make an important decision about our life as a couple. It may be that it is necessary to decide on the next step in our relationship, such as getting engaged or taking a step towards cohabitation or marriage. This card reminds us that we must take into account both our personal needs and those of our partner, and that we must make a conscious and mature decision.

In general, The Lovers is a card that reminds us of the importance of making conscious choices in our love relationships. It emphasizes that

we must choose wisely and weigh the consequences of our decisions, and that we must take into account both our personal needs and those of our partner in order to establish and/or maintain a balanced and harmonious relationship.

If it is inverted, this card indicates a break in relationships, divorce, unhappy love, making a bad decision. It warns us against debauchery and letting ourselves be seduced by bad people. If anything, it suggests a period of emotional instability and uncertainty, perhaps a love triangle that strains a relationship.

VII. The Chariot

DIVINATORY MEANING
Triumph, victory, overcoming obstacles, ambition, conquest. Great self-control, ability to determine one's own destiny. Speed, hyperactivity. Journey. Expense or profit, movement of funds.

INVERTED
Conflict, litigation, failure, loss. Situation dangerously out of control. Lack of tact, unjustified ambition. Bad behavior. Activity feverish and without rest. Danger of a violent accident. Disease. Trip canceled.

The Chariot is a card that is often interpreted as the symbol of victory, power of advance and control. In the context of love, this card can indicate that we are moving towards a new stage in our love life and that we have the determination and ability necessary to achieve our goals.

If we are alone, The Chariot can indicate that this is a good time to advance to achieve our love goals and seek a new relationship. This card reminds us that we must be daring and trust our abilities to attract the person we long for. The symbology of this card is clear, the character in The Chariot is in a triumphal procession, celebrating his conquest; so this card can suggest a seduction or a conquest (if it were next to the Seven of Swords, it would suggest an affair). In any case, the message is let's keep moving.

On the other hand, if we are in a relationship, The Chariot can indicate that we are not stagnant, but that our relationship is evolving. It may be that we are committing more in the relationship or moving towards living together. The card reminds us that we must have confidence in ourselves and in our partner to achieve the proposed goals together. Let us note that the chariot is drawn by two horses, which, like the members of a couple, must act in common agreement in order to move forward.

In general, The Chariot is a card that emphasizes the importance of having confidence in ourselves and in our love relationships. It reminds us that we must move forward with determination and discipline to achieve our love goals and succeed in our relationships. It also teaches us that, in order to establish and carry out any intimate relationship, it is necessary to act in common agreement and have common goals. If the

two horses who haul the chariot pull in opposite directions, the chariot will stop.

If it is inverted, this card indicates lack of control, arrogance, and inability to relate to other people on an equal footing. If we do not moderate our behavior, and we are already in a relationship, we will run the risk of spoiling it. Unless we learn to cooperate with the people around us, we will not be able to carry out any common project.

VIII. Justice (XI in RWS)

DIVINATORY MEANING
Justice will be done. To maintain balance certain things must be sacrificed, adjustment is necessary. Integrity, firm purpose, judging action, moderation in all things. Clarity of judgment. It may be related to legal matters: lawsuit won, divorce, etc. Action rational and according to the rules.

INVERTED
Injustice. Abuse of power, fanaticism, harsh judge. Wrongful conviction, false accusations, lawsuit, process, scam. Weakness, loss, insecurity, uncertainty. A pathological need to control everything. Critical and condemning attitude.

Justice is a card that is often interpreted as representing equity, fairness, and balance. In the context of love, this card can indicate that we are at a time when it is important to balance our personal needs with those of our partner in order to have a harmonious and just relationship. Alternatively — if other cards support this interpretation — this card can also indicate divorce.

If we are alone, Justice can indicate that we need to find the right balance in our love life. It may be that we are being too demanding with our potential partners or that we are accepting less than we deserve. Justice reminds us that we must be fair both with ourselves and with others, and seek a relationship in which both parties can balance their needs.

On the other hand, if we are in a relationship, Justice can indicate that this is a good time to balance our needs with those of our partner. It may be necessary to discuss important issues such as trust, commitment, or loyalty, and find a fair balance that works for both partners. This card suggests that we should be fair and understanding with our partner, and be attentive to their needs and desires. To achieve justice we may need to make some sacrifices or adjustments.

In general, Justice is a card that reminds us of the importance of finding balance and justice in our love relationships. It reminds us to be fair and just to ourselves and others, and to seek relationships that are harmonious and balanced. It also reminds us that we must listen to our partner

and be understanding of their needs and desires, to achieve a fair balance in our relationship.

If it is inverted, this card indicates a severe imbalance in our relationship. A hostile divorce, with possible loss of property, if other cards confirm it. It is advisable that we moderate our expectations and claims; let's not demand too much of our partner, but also, on the other hand, we should take all possible precautions to protect ourselves.

IX. The Hermit

DIVINATORY MEANING
Search for spiritual understanding. Concentration on a clear purpose. Wisdom, silence, patience, discretion (the same four virtues possessed by the second major arcana, The High Priestess). Withdrawal from the world, continence, austerity, prudence. Pilgrimage, meditation, study, meeting with a teacher; it can be an expert or adviser in a certain area, spiritual or material. Experienced doctor.

INVERTED
Closed and reclusive attitude, shy, misanthropic. Fixed ideas. Excessive caution and distrust. Search for defects and critique of everything. Suppression of desires. Sadness, poverty, greed. Hidden enemies, dark cabal.

The Hermit is a card that is often seen as the symbol of introspection, solitude, and wisdom. In the context of love, this card can indicate that we are at a time when we need time to reflect on our lives and seek answers within ourselves, away from the social scene.

If we are single, The Hermit may indicate that we need to focus on our own personal and spiritual growth, which will help us be more prepared to have better social relationships. This is not a time to seek new love relationships, but to cultivate our own self. May be we should look for spiritual guidance.

On the other hand, if we are in a relationship, The Hermit suggests a period of withdrawal and introspection. It is important to be honest with ourselves and with our partner and keep the communication channels open, to make clear that we need time for ourselves, to find our own way.

In general, The Hermit, on the subject of love, tells us that we are in a period of introspection, of little social life. In fact, The Hermit suggests continence and austerity. That does not mean that we cannot have satisfactory relationships, but, in case of having an intimate relationship, this card indicates a certain cooling off and distance.

When it is inverted, The Hermit suggests a certain level of mistrust (even paranoia), misanthropy, repression of feelings and refusal to accept reality and therefore some neglect of both our own well-being and

that of our partner (if we have one). Actually, being reversed, this card rather suggests loneliness and misogyny.

X. The Wheel of Fortune

DIVINATORY MEANING
The cycles of life, change, luck and destiny. Good fortune, luck smiles on us and we know how to take advantage of it. Sound, balanced judgment. Liveliness, good cheer. For a wedding: activates its realization.

INVERTED
Carelessness, speculation, gambling, leaving things to chance, insecurity, lack of seriousness, improvidence, bohemian character. Unstable situation, sudden change, profit and loss. Being at the mercy of the fluctuations of fortune.

The Wheel of Fortune is a card that indicates the cycles of life, change and luck. In the context of love, this card can indicate that we are experiencing a major change in our love life, and that luck will favor us.

If we are alone, The Wheel of Fortune suggests that this is a good time to seek a new relationship. This card reminds us that we must be open to the opportunities that arise in our love life, to take advantage of luck, which is on our side. It can also indicate that we need to leave behind relationships from the past that no longer serve us and move on towards a new cycle in our love life.

On the other hand, if we are in a relationship, The Wheel of Fortune can indicate a major change in it. We may be going through ups and downs, our relationship may not be stable, but The Wheel of Fortune reminds us that luck is in our favor and that it is important to maintain a positive attitude to overcome these ups and downs. It also tells us that we need to be vigilant so as not to miss out on the new cycles and opportunities that arise in our relationship, and to be willing to adapt to the changes in our love life.

In general, The Wheel of Fortune is a card that reminds us of the importance of being open to change and to take the opportunities that appear in our love relationships. It reminds us that luck can favor us, but that we must be prepared to face the cycles of life and adapt to the changes that arise in our love life. To take advantage of the opportunities that present themselves, we must maintain a positive attitude and have confidence in ourselves and in our ability to overcome difficult moments in

our love relationships. Let's remember that although we can lose some things, new opportunities can also present themselves.

If inverted, this card indicates that we are neglecting our relationships and our lives, that we leave everything to chance and are incapable of planning or ordering our existence. The situation is not stable, our love life will experience unpredictable ups and downs.

XI. Strength (VIII in RWS)

DIVINATORY MEANING
Sublimation or regulation of passions and base instincts. Power, energy. The spirit that dominates matter. Action, courage, success. Strong will and great physical strength. Power over animals. The Chariot shows us the masculine will in action, here we see a feminine influence that tames rather than overwhelms.

INVERTED
Lack of self-control. Abuse of power, violent domination, cruelty, fight. Immorality, insensitivity, recklessness, rudeness, callousness. Doubts, weakness, a pathological need to control everything.

Strength tells us that we have a great power of attraction, that we know how to translate our desires into actions without forcing anyone, winning over others, but without abusing them.

If we are alone, Strength suggests that we must dare to leave our comfort zone and seek new opportunities in love. This card reminds us that we must trust ourselves and our abilities to find happiness in a relationship. It can also indicate that we need to work on our self-esteem and self-confidence in order to attract a suitable partner for us.

On the other hand, if we are in a relationship, Strength teaches us that we should to show firm determination and fight to keep our relationship in good shape, as well as self-control, so as not to abuse anyone. We may be facing challenges, but this card reminds us that we have the inner and outer strength to overcome them. It can also indicate that we need to be more passionate and show our love and commitment to our partner.

In general, Strength is a card that reminds us of the importance of having self-control and courage to face challenges in our love relationships. It tells us that we must trust ourselves and our abilities to find happiness in a relationship, and that we must be passionate and committed in our love life. It also teaches us that we should not abuse the power of seduction that we have.

When inverted, Strength indicates extreme selfishness, lack of self-control, and a choleric temperament. When our passions are out of control we run the risk of abusing others; it is imperative that we moderate ourselves and curb our low instincts.

XII. The Hanged Man

DIVINATORY MEANING
Introspection, patience, renunciation, self-denial; loss of ego, a period in limbo between significant events, suspension of all action, indecision; transition; search for a new path; sacrifice; repentance. To be in the pillory, ridicule, to be exposed. Visionary, prophet.

INVERTED
Isolation. Dreamer lost in the clouds, his visions will not come true. Lack of sacrifice; inability to give what is needed; selfishness. Wasted effort, failure.

In the context of love, The Hanged Man can indicate that we are going through a period of waiting or sacrifice in our love life.

If we are alone, The Hanged Man can indicate that we need to take some time to reflect and evaluate what we really want in a relationship. This card reminds us that sometimes it is necessary to make sacrifices in love, and that being alone for a while can be beneficial if we take advantage of that time to grow spiritually. It can also indicate that we need to let go of negative patterns in our past relationships in order to move towards a healthier relationship.

On the other hand, if we are in a relationship, The Hanged Man can indicate that we need to take some time to meditate on our relationship and make some changes. It may be that we are experiencing a difficult period, but The Hanged Man teaches us that sometimes it is necessary to make sacrifices to achieve a stronger and lasting relationship. It can also indicate that we need to be more patient and wait for things to settle in our interpersonal relationships.

In general, The Hanged Man is a card that emphasizes the importance of reflection and sacrifice in our love relationships. It reminds us that sometimes it is necessary to take some time to evaluate what we really want in a relationship and make some changes to achieve a healthier relationship. It also teaches us that sometimes it is necessary to be patient and wait for things to work out in our relationships, even if it means sacrificing or putting something off in the present moment.

If it is inverted, The Hanged Man indicates that we have a tendency to delay what we should do, leaving everything for tomorrow, indulging in

gratifying illusions in the short term, which serve us no useful purpose. If we fail to overcome our selfishness and inertia, our relationships will not prosper.

XIII. Death[2]

DIVINATORY MEANING
Complete transformation. Death and rebirth. The end of something Renewal of ideas, profitable change. The loss of some things. Distancing, dispersion of affections, a feeling, a hope will be uprooted.

INVERTED
Stagnation, failed marriage, lack of opportunities, death, broken hope, dream, petrification. Melancholy, mourning, sadness, disappointment. Decay, decomposition, corruption.

The Death card can intimidate many people, since one of its meanings is physical death. In the context of love, this card can indicate the end of a relationship or a major transformation of it.

If we are alone, Death can indicate that we are experiencing a stage of important changes in our love life. It is possible that we have gone through a recent breakup. Death reminds us that sometimes it is necessary to let go of what no longer serves us in order to open up to new opportunities for love. It can also indicate that we are ready for a transformation in our love lives and that it is time to seek more meaningful relationships.

If we are in a relationship, Death can indicate that we are experiencing major changes in our relationship. It may be that we are going through a crisis or that we are reconsidering the perspectives of our relationship. Death reminds us that sometimes it is necessary to let go of what no longer works in a relationship in order to transform it and make it stronger. Also, in other cases it may indicate that we have insurmountable differences with our partner, or possibly we are involved in a stale relationship that is better to leave behind.

In general, Death is a card that reminds us of the importance of change and transformation in our love relationships. It teaches us that it is necessary to let go of what no longer serves us and transform our relationships to make them more meaningful and satisfying. It also tells us that it is important to be open to the new and not accept a mediocre relationship, if we want to achieve the happiness and satisfaction we seek.

---

2   Unnamed card in the Marseille Tarot.

When reversed, Death indicates a period of stagnation, when no hope comes to fruition, and we withdraw into ourselves. It also suggests a marriage or relationship that has been spoiled.

XIV. Temperance

Divinatory Meaning
Moderation, sobriety, economy, frugality, patience, adaptation, accommodating character. Composure, self-control, reflection. Combination of opposites, mixture of the past and the present. Good marriage or relationship with others. Slow progress.

Inverted
Lack of control, intemperance, excesses, conflict. Emotional ups and downs. Chance of shipwreck. Laziness, apathy, indecision, abandonment, letting go. Submission to fashion, prejudices or beliefs. Priest, religion, sect. Spinning around without being able to move forward.

In the context of love, Temperance can indicate that we need to find balance and harmony in our love relationships, and that it is important for us to live in harmony with everyone, and that we almost always succeed in some way.

If we are alone, Temperance indicates that this is a period where it is important to avoid all conflict, and to be tolerant of the peculiarities of others. This card indicates a slow but sure evolution, and assures us that sooner or later we will be able to establish a loving relationship that fill us with satisfaction. It may be that we are looking for a meaningful relationship, but we also need time to ourselves and to develop our own interests. Temperance reminds us that it is important to be patient and to find a balance in our love life in order to achieve a healthy and fulfilling relationship.

If we are in a relationship, Temperance may indicate that we need to improve the balance and harmony of it. It may be that we are going through a difficult period, but it is important to be patient and maintain balance, in order to achieve a stronger and more lasting relationship. It can also indicate that we need to be more tolerant and understanding with our partner in order to achieve a more harmonious relationship.

In general, Temperance is a card that reminds us of the importance of achieving a good balance and harmony in our love relationships. It teaches us that it is important to be patient and tolerant with our partner in order to achieve a healthy and satisfying relationship. It also emphasizes that it is important to maintain the proper balance between

our personal needs and the needs of our partner in order to achieve a more fulfilling love life.

When reversed, Temperance suggests imbalance and interpersonal conflict. It is a sign that we do not take good care of keeping our relationships in good condition. If our temperament is variable and we are capricious, we will not be able to establish or maintain good relationships of any kind. If we want to enjoy the friendship and love of other people, we had better have a little moderation and sobriety; let's put some order in our lives and be more tolerant with others. Also it may mean that we are easily influenced for others, instead we should be tolerant with others, but keep our own counsel.

XV. The Devil

Divinatory Meaning
Force majeure, fatality. Vehemence, passion and desire, blind impulse. Power of seduction, great ability to influence others, black magic. Temptation, addiction, selfishness. Chained to a bad relationship. Sadism, malevolence, sexual deviation, uncontrolled carnal passions.

Inverted
Release of ties; overcoming materialism, pride and self-interest. Truce, shyness, indecision.

In the context of love, The Devil can indicate a relationship based on extreme dependency, excessive control or an obsessive one.

Although The Devil generally indicates bad influences (both from people, as well as from obsessions or vices that we may have, like drugs or alcohol), on the other hand it is also related to irresistible influences, which in the Tarot are called force majeure, that is, a unforeseeable and unavoidable circumstance that prevents us from doing something or forces us to follow a certain course of action; so such force is not necessarily bad, just irresistible. That is to say that The Devil can also indicate the force of destiny, something that we cannot control. That "something" can be a passion that arises within us or an external influence.

If we are alone, The Devil can indicate that we repeat unhealthy patterns in our love relationships. It may be that we are looking for a relationship based on passion and intensity, but we find ourselves attracted to people who do not suit us. This card reminds us that it is important to be careful in our loving choices and avoid toxic relationships, which harm us in the long term.

If we are already in a relationship, The Devil can indicate that we are experiencing control issues or extreme dependency in our relationship. It could be that our partner is trying to control us or that we feel trapped in an unhealthy relationship. The Devil reminds us that it is important to take steps to set healthy boundaries in our relationships and avoid extreme behavior lifestyles.

In general, The Devil is a card that reminds us of the importance of being aware of our choices in our relationships and avoid unhealthy affairs based on addiction or extreme dependency. It reminds us that it

is important to set boundaries in our relationships and avoid unhealthy patterns that can lead to an unfulfilling and toxic relationship.

If it is inverted, this card indicates that we are overcoming unhealthy behavior patterns and freeing ourselves from toxic relationships. It also teaches us that we can leave pride and selfishness behind. It is possible that after ending a toxic relationship, we go through a period of indecision, until we find the path to a fuller life again.

XVI. The Tower

DIVINATORY MEANING
Catastrophe, collapse, ruin. Escape from prison or release from bondage, relationship breakup, divorce. Bankruptcy, hardship. Accident, sudden death. Punishment resulting from pride or excesses committed. The plans will fail. The "finger of God."

INVERTED
Limitations. Trapped in an unhappy situation. Routinary life, continued oppression. False accusations, prison.

The Tower is often associated with unexpected and drastic events that change our life. In the context of love, this card can indicate a sudden change or crisis in a relationship.

If we are alone, The Tower can indicate that we are going through a period when our expectations and the structure we give to our lives are being shaken. It may be that some project or element that supports us is falling apart, or that we are going through some kind of hardship. This is not the best time to build new relationships. The best thing we can do in times of crisis like this is to try to moderate our pretensions and be realistic. When the commotion passes we will see everything more clearly.

If we are in a relationship, The Tower can indicate a crisis or a sudden change in the relationship. It could mean an unexpected separation or divorce, or it could be that a sudden revelation causes a change in the dynamics of the relationship. The Tower reminds us that it is important to be open to changes and adapt to new circumstances.

In general, The Tower reminds us that life is unpredictable and that sudden and unexpected changes can occur in our love relationships. It is important to be able to cope with possible crises and adapt to new circumstances in order to have healthier and more satisfying relationships. The Tower also teaches us that it is important to be honest and sincere in our relationships, putting pride aside, to avoid unpleasant surprises or sudden crises. In this case we could remember the phrase "better safe than sorry," although if The Tower appears in a reading, it may already be too late for that. On the other hand, The Tower also means liberation

from ties, therefore, if we are tied to a toxic relationship, this card can have a positive meaning.

If it is inverted, The Tower indicates an unsatisfactory relationship, which we cannot improve or abandon. It can also suggest inability to share our own feelings and to communicate with other people; low emotional intelligence.

XVII. The Star

DIVINATORY MEANING
Insight and clarity of vision, inspiration, ray of light. Your hopes will be fulfilled. Unexpected help. The gifts of the spirit, flexibility. Purity, naturalness, honesty. Totally spiritual card.

INVERTED
Arrogance, pessimism, stubbornness, error in judgment and/or perception. Restructuring, deprivation and abandonment. Your hopes will not be fulfilled.

In the context of love, The Star promises us that our hopes will be fulfilled, and teaches us that if we are sincere and open to the spiritual influences, we will be blessed and we will have a beneficial effect on the lives of those around us.

If we are alone, The Star can indicate that we are experiencing a moment of inspiration and renewal in our life, with great mental clarity, which can positively affect our love life. It may be that we feel more optimistic and hopeful about finding our ideal partner, or perhaps we are overcoming trauma from the past, which will allow us to be more open to love. The Star reminds us that it is important to trust our own abilities and keep hope in love, even if we have had painful experiences. We may find a great love.

If we are in a relationship, The Star tells us that we have excellent communication and communion of feelings with our partner. As long as we keep the communication channels open and mutual trust endures, we will have a healthy and satisfying relationship. Also means that we are full of hope and plans for the future.

In general, The Star is a card that reminds us of the importance of not giving up hope and having faith in love. It teaches us that it is possible to overcome obstacles and heal the wounds of the past to have healthier and more satisfying relationships. It also reminds us that it is important to be honest, communicate well and have confidence in our partner, in order to have strong and lasting relationships.

When inverted, The Star indicates bad communication and pride that prevents us from perceiving our partner's true needs. It indicates unsatisfactory and ephemeral relationships. In this case, the best thing we

can do is seek a more spiritual life, leaving behind selfishness and materialism.

XVIII. The Moon

DIVINATORY MEANING
Threshold of an important change, a difficult and confusing path. Painful exploration of one's own dark side or the psychic domain, psychoanalysis. Imagination, instinct, mystery, intense dreams, nightmares. Possible error and/or deception.

INVERTED
Vague and disturbing feelings. Emotional ups and downs. Depression. Unseen dangers and/or enemies. Can't find the way, retreat. Hallucination, delusion, hysteria, paranoia. It is recommended to avoid risks. Accompanied by IX, The Hermit: Scandal, denunciation and defamation.

The Moon is often associated with intuition, imagination, and hidden mysteries. In the context of love, this card can indicate confusion or uncertainty in relationships.

If we are alone, The Moon can indicate that our relationships are unclear or ambiguous. It may be that we are not sure what we want in a relationship, or it may be that we are experiencing a strong attraction to someone who confuses us. The Moon reminds us that it is important to trust our intuition and listen to our own feelings in order to find the clarity we seek.

If we are in a relationship, The Moon can indicate that we are experiencing a stage of confusion or uncertainty with our partner. It could be that there are hidden secrets or mysteries that are affecting our relationship, or it could be that we feel insecure about our partner. The Moon reminds us that it is important to be honest, both with ourselves and with our partner to clear up any misunderstanding or confusion in the relationship.

In general, The Moon is a card that teaches us the importance of trusting our intuition and our feelings to find clarity in love relationships. It suggests that there may be hidden secrets or mysteries that we must clarify in order to have healthier and more satisfying relationships. It also emphasizes that it is important to be honest and sincere in our relationships to avoid confusion and uncertainty.

If The Moon is inverted, the confusion is amplified. We may become a toy of our emotions and fears, but there is also the possibility that we are being cheated on by our partner or by another person. This is not a good time to make important decisions, due to the lack of clarity and the disturbing feelings that plague us. To gain some insight, the best thing we can do is stop and seek the help of someone we can trust, be it a spiritual teacher, a psychologist, or just a trusted friend.

XIX. The Sun

DIVINATORY MEANING
Good reputation, fame, charisma. Triumph and success assured. Lucid discernment, clarity of judgment and expression, literary or artistic talent. Brotherhood, marital happiness. Healing, physical or emotional.

INVERTED
Immaturity. Difficulty facing reality. A pretentious nobody. Confusion, vanity, pretense, false pomp, boasting, pride, egocentrism. Lost relationship, marriage or job. Canceled plans.

The Sun represents joy and vitality. In the context of love, this card suggests that we are experiencing a phase of happiness and fulfillment in our love relationships.

If we are alone, The Sun can indicate that we are feeling happy and confident in ourselves, and that we project well socially, which will allow us to attract positive and fulfilling love relationships. This card suggests that we are ready to find a partner who shares our values and makes us feel fulfilled, as indicated by the playful pair of children shown on the card (at least in the Marseille Tarot, the RWS Tarot shows a child on a horse, as a symbol of joy and freedom).

If we are in a relationship, The Sun suggests an expansive and happy phase, with excellent communication. This card reflects a flourishing couple relationship, with a great amount of energy and vitality, which allows us to enjoy the intimacy, passion and harmony of our relationship with our partner.

In general, The Sun is a very positive card that indicates a phase of happiness and fulfillment in our love relationships. This card suggests that we are on the right track and that our love life is positive and healthy. It is important to remember that this card also reminds us that we must continue to work on ourselves and our social relationships in order to maintain happiness and harmony in the long term.

If it is inverted, The Sun indicates that it is difficult for us to connect with other people due to our immaturity, and perhaps because we have excessive pretensions. If we are in a relationship, we should do every-

thing possible to take care of it, because the inverted Sun is a bad omen for love relationships.

XX. Judgment

DIVINATORY MEANING
Radical change, new opportunity, reintegration, reconciliation. Spiritual awakening, enlightenment. Revealed secrets. Favorable judicial opinion.

INVERTED
Mistake. Spiritual vacillation, fear, weakness, guilt, separation, divorce. Decision postponed. Adverse judicial opinion.

In the context of love, Judgment suggests that we are going through a phase of clarity and renewal in our love relationships.

If we are alone, Judgment can indicate that past love relationships can be revived, to offer us a new opportunity. It also indicates new possibilities, so it is important that we are open to new experiences and new people that may appear in our lives.

If we are in a relationship, Judgment suggests that we are in a phase of renewal and clarity in our life as a couple. It may be that we have gone through a period of confusion or uncertainty in our relationship, but now we have more clarity and understanding, perhaps we see our relationship from a different angle that makes us enjoy it more and feel a renewed passion. This card suggests that it is important to take into account our past experiences to make wiser decisions in our social and loving relationships.

In general, Judgment is a card that reminds us of the importance of being open to new experiences and new — or renewed — loving relationships. This card teaches us that it is important to let go of old ways of thinking and habits that no longer serve us. It also reminds us that it is important to learn from our past experiences in order to make wise decisions in our current and future love relationships.

If this card is inverted, it can indicate divorce, separation; doubts and confusion, which will make us make mistakes that can harm our relationships.

XX

· LE · IVGEMENT ·

XXI. The World

DIVINATORY MEANING
Realization, completed work, rewards, security, very favorable circumstances. Travel, emigration (within the same continent), change of place of residence. Buying and selling of lands.

INVERTED
Obstacles, stagnation, hindrances, lack of vision, failure, disappointment. Hostile atmosphere. Fear of change or travel, being too attached to the place of residence or work.

In the context of love, The World suggests that we are experiencing a phase of completion and culmination in our love relationships.

If we are alone, The World can indicate that we are in a phase of personal fulfillment in which we feel complete and happy with ourselves. This card suggests material abundance and a secure situation, which makes it easier for us to establish loving relationships that complement us and make us feel fulfilled in all aspects of our lives.

If we are in a relationship, The World indicates an expansive phase, with a lot of movement. It is possible that we are carrying out common projects with our partner, oriented towards the outside world, such as looking for a new home or planning a memorable vacation. This is an excellent time to carry out all kinds of plans, as a family.

In general, The World is a very positive card that indicates a period of realization and culmination in love relationships. This card suggests that we enjoy balance and happiness in our relationships, and that if we are alone, we are ready to attract positive and fulfilling love relationships.

If this card is inverted, it means that our love life is blocked or stagnant. At the moment we will not be offered opportunities, but we are not taking care of renewing or improving our love life either, because we are reluctant to change and we are too attached to the past.

Minor Arcana: Wands

Ace of Wands

DIVINATORY MEANING
Creation. Initiative and determination. Ability to carry out ventures. Beginning of a company, adventure, invention or something new. Energy, enthusiasm. Good health, virility and fertility. Conception or birth of a child.

INVERTED
Fall. Lose or postpone something (employment, business, etc.). False starts. Impotence, lack of energy, lack of drive.

The Ace of Wands indicates that we are experiencing a phase of passion and enthusiasm in our love relationships. It also suggests virility and fertility and — if confirmed by other cards — the conception or birth of a child.

If we are alone, the Ace of Wands can indicate that we are in a phase of new beginnings in love. This card suggests that we are full of energy and passion, ready to explore new opportunities in love. It is possible that we experience an increase in our self-confidence and that we are willing to take risks in love to find the happiness and satisfaction that we seek.

If we are in a relationship, the Ace of Wands suggests that our passion and energy have increased. We may be planning new adventures as a couple or exploring new ways to keep the passion alive. One of the meanings of this card is conception, birth, so it is a good omen for those who want to have children.

In general, the Ace of Wands is a very positive card that indicates a phase of passion and new beginnings in love relationships. This card suggests that we are full of energy and enthusiasm, ready to explore new opportunities in love to find happiness and fulfillment in our lives.

If the card is inverted, it indicates depression, impotence, lack of drive. It is possible that our passion has weakened and we do not pay much attention to our partner, nor do we have the will to start new relationships.

Two of Wands

DIVINATORY MEANING
Initiative, planning and projection of power, increasing influence; maturity, personality, courage, willpower. Crossroads, several options to choose from.

INVERTED
Disturbance, surprise. Restlessness, fear, loss of faith in oneself. Illness, physical suffering. The good streak ended.

The Two of Wands is a card that indicates decision making and exploring new opportunities. In the context of love, this card suggests that we are exploring options and considering different paths in our love life.

If we are alone, the Two of Wands can indicate that we are considering different options in love. We may be deciding if we want to be in a relationship or if we prefer to focus on our career or other aspects of our life. This card suggests that we have many alternatives available and we are in a position to make informed decisions about our life, both in the field of love as in general.

If we are in a relationship, the Two of Wands can indicate that we are exploring new ways to strengthen our relationship, or that it has matured and we are ready to take it to the next level. We may be considering a major change like moving in with our partner or committing more seriously to each other. This card suggests that we are in a phase of making important decisions and that we have the power to shape our relationship in the direction we want.

In general, the Two of Wands suggests that we are in a phase of exploration and decision making in our love life. This card suggests that we have several options available to us and that we have the power to choose the path our love life will follow. It is important to remember that this card also reminds us that we must remain true to ourselves and our values in love in order to achieve fulfilling relationships in the long term.

If the Two of Wands is inverted, it suggests problems in our social relationships. We no longer know clearly what we want, and our immaturity will not allow us to make the right decisions, so our relationships will suffer.

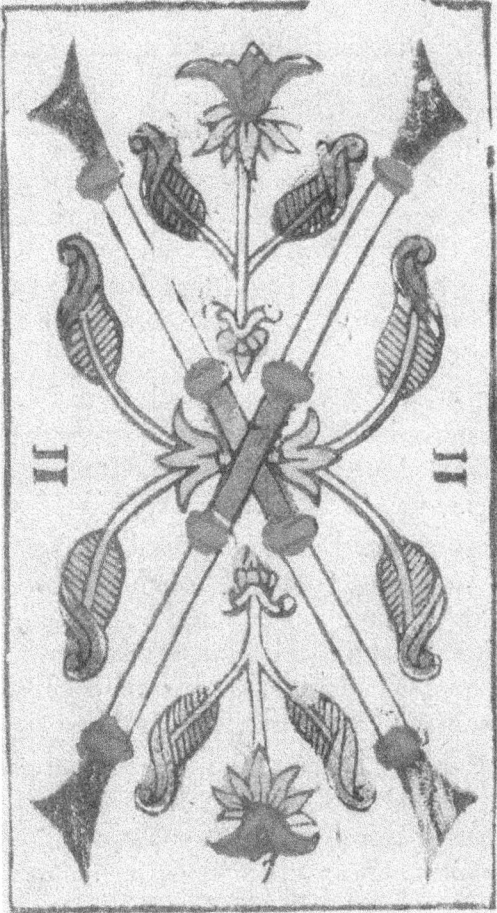

Three of Wands

DIVINATORY MEANING
Established and expanding force or company, goals achieved. Wealth, power, courage, perseverance, pride, nobility. Cooperation, partnership. Warning against pride and arrogance.

INVERTED
Inconsistency, failed plans, disappointment, arduous complications, withdrawal, interruption. Theft, deceit, loss.

The Three of Wands is a card that represents consolidation, expansion and the search for new opportunities. In the context of love, this card suggests that we are expanding our horizons and exploring new possibilities in our love life. The Three of Wands also indicates that we occupy a prominent position on the social scene and it warns us against pride and arrogance.

If we are alone, the Three of Wands can indicate that we are expanding our social circle and opening our minds to new people and experiences. We may be dating and meeting new people, even those we might not have considered before.

If we are in a relationship, the Three of Wands teaches us that it is important to share common activities with our loved ones and make decisions together, without imposing our ideas on our partner. It is important to maintain the health of the intimate relationships that we have; even though we have an intense work life, we must still dedicate the best of ourselves to our family and our loved ones.

In general, the Three of Wands suggests that we are opening our horizons and learning to share our life with our loved ones. This card suggests that we are in a phase of expansion and growth, and that there are many exciting opportunities available to us, but it also warns us not to become conceited or have an inflated idea of ourselves.

When it is inverted, the Three of Wands indicates complications and disappointments in our social life and our intimate relationships. Someone close to us may disappoint us and we may have to postpone certain things. The best thing we can do to get through this period of uncertainty is to keep our lines of communication open with our loved ones.

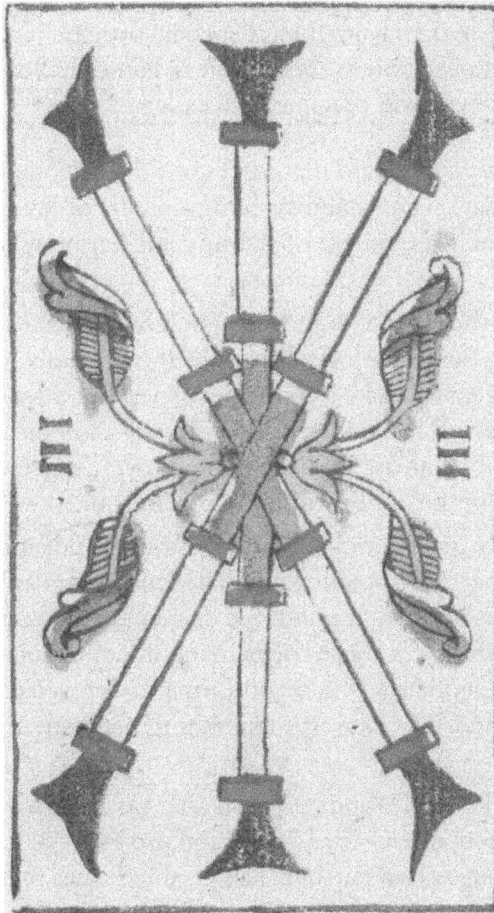

Four of Wands

DIVINATORY MEANING
Consummation, prosperity, celebration. Settlement, peace, harmony. Romance, marriage, partnership.

INVERTED
It has a similar meaning as when it appears upright, but less fully and with imperfections. Doubts, nervousness, contradictions, incomplete happiness. Excesses will precipitate decadence.

The Four of Wands is a card that represents the celebration of achievements, consolidation and stability. In the context of love, this card suggests that we are in a moment of stability and harmony in our love and family life.

If we are alone, the Four of Wands is a good omen regarding the formation of intimate bonds with other people. If we already have a relationship, we may be able to take it to the next level, but if we don't, it promises us that love will come into our life. In any case, this card indicates that we are well balanced and in harmony with ourselves, so we can make good use of the opportunities that come our way.

If we are already in a relationship, the Four of Wands indicates that we are enjoying a period of stability and harmony. It is possible that we are celebrating some important milestone or event in our relationship, such as an anniversary, or perhaps formalizing it, contemplating marriage. This card suggests that this is a good time to appreciate and celebrate what we have and take care of maintaining harmony in our relationships.

In general, the Four of Wands suggests that we are in a moment of stability and harmony in our love, social and professional life, whether we are alone or living with a partner. This card indicates that this is a good time to enjoy and appreciate the love we have in our lives and celebrate our blessings.

If it is inverted, the Four of Wands warns us against excesses in our interpersonal relationships. It is advisable to do everything possible to preserve harmony in our social and family life and seek balance. We must not take the well-being we enjoy for granted, if we do not take care of our loved ones or if we are excessively ambitious we will harm our-

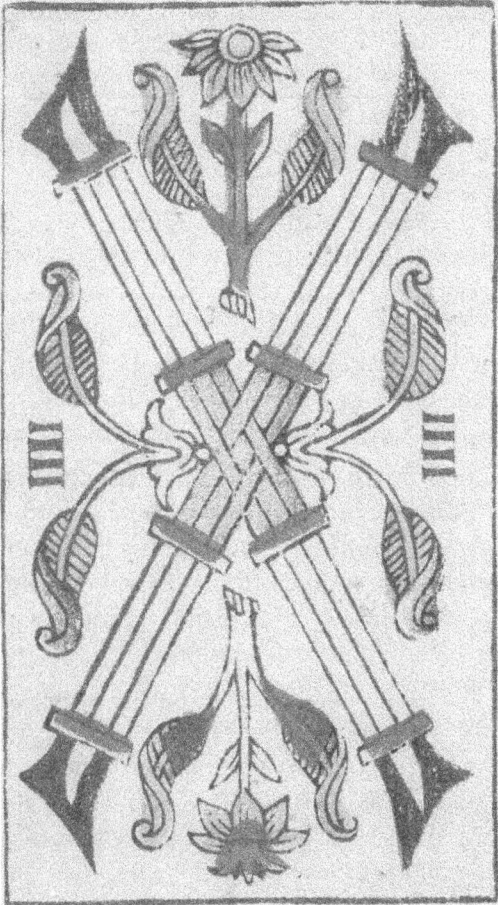

selves and those around us. Let us be tolerant with others and refrain from committing excesses.

Five of Wands

DIVINATORY MEANING
Conflict, complications, entanglement. Quarrel, violent fight, stormy discussion. Competition, obstacles, opposition. Litigation.

INVERTED
Revenue. New business opportunities. Victory after overcoming opposition.

In the context of love, the Five of Wands suggests that we are facing conflict or challenges in our love life.

If we are alone, the Five of Wands can indicate competition or rivalry in our relationships. It is possible that we are attracted to someone who is already in a relationship or that there are other people who are interested in the same person as us. This card suggests that we must be prepared to fight for what we want in love and be willing to compete for the attention of the person we are interested in.

If we are in a relationship, the Five of Wands suggests that we are experiencing some conflict with our partner, perhaps competing for control or having intense disagreements. This card teaches us that we must find a way to overcome the conflict, either reaching an agreement, or trying to see the situation from a different angle, without prejudice. If both parties want to find a solution, it is worth the effort of working together to resolve disagreements and find solutions.

In general, the Five of Wands suggests that we are experiencing challenges and conflicts in our love life. This card tells us that we must be prepared to fight for love and be willing to compete for the attention and love of the person we are interested in. If we are already in a relationship, this card teaches us that we should try to resolve conflicts and work together to find solutions.

If the Five of Wands is inverted, it indicates that the conflicts are going to be resolved or overcome, and harmony will once again prevail in our relationships.

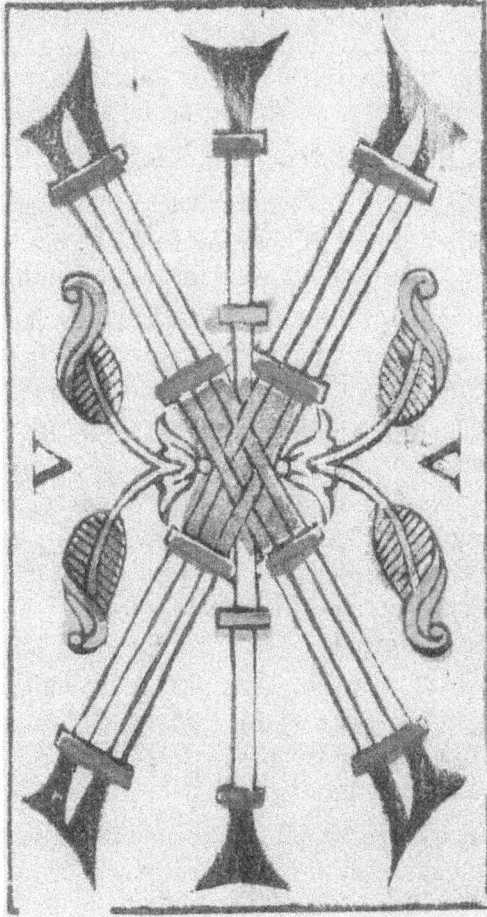

Six of Wands

DIVINATORY MEANING
Victory after a fight. Good news, progress, advance. Leadership, support from friends or followers. Alliance.

INVERTED
It is not possible to form an alliance, or your adversaries ally against you. Someone triumphs at your expense. Lack of recognition. Postponement. Insolence of the victorious. Betrayal, apprehension.

The Six of Wands is a card that indicates victory and success after a fight or challenge. In the context of love, this card suggests that we are in a good moment and that we are moving forward in our love life.

If we are alone, the Six of Wands indicates that we will gain the trust of the person we are interested in, probably with the help of a third party. This is a good time to go ahead and express our feelings, since we are likely to succeed in our attempt, and not only the partner we are looking for, but also their family, will welcome us.

If we are already in a relationship, the Six of Wands suggests a period of excellent communication and cooperation with our partner, after having overcome a challenge together. This card tells us that this is a good time to celebrate the success achieved and enjoy the harmony and consolidation of our relationship.

In general, the Six of Wands suggests that we are being successful and moving forward in our love life. This card tells us that it is a good time to go ahead and express our feelings to the person we are interested in, or to celebrate and enjoy the relationship we currently have.

When it is inverted, the Six of Wands indicates disagreements with our partner and our family. It is a period of our life in which we find ourselves isolated and worried. It can also indicate that another person takes away the person we love (if this card is flanked by the Seven of Swords there would be no doubt about it).

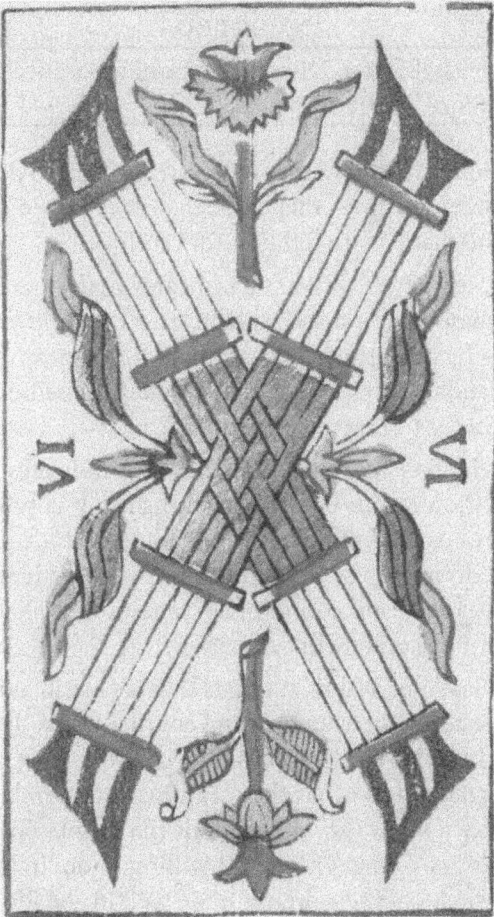

Seven of Wands

DIVINATORY MEANING
Firm determination. Victory through courage despite the odds. Effort, struggle, fierce competition. Firm stand in the face of opposition. Negotiation, discussion, contract.

INVERTED
Inability to face challenges. Disorganization, ignorance or lack of will that leads to failure. Embarrassment.

The Seven of Wands is a card that represents a fight to defend what we want. In the context of love, this card suggests that we are in a defensive position and that we are fighting for our love.

If we are alone, the Seven of Wands indicates that we are struggling to find love. We may be at a disadvantage, and the only way we can get what we want is by accepting a compromise. That doesn't mean we have to lower our standards, but rather that we have to be both persevering and flexible in order to achieve our goals.

If we are in a relationship, the Seven of Wands indicates that we are in a defensive position in our current relationship. It is possible that our partner pressures us to obtain certain advantages or achieve something with which we do not agree. It is important that, without abandoning our position, we reach some kind of agreement that allows us to overcome the current disagreement.

In general, the Seven of Wands suggests that we are in a defensive position and that we can only overcome the conflict that afflicts us through negotiation. When there are discussions, in order to reach a deal that allows both parties to get what they want, without embarrassing anyone, it is necessary to be very clear about the points on which we can offer concessions, and what we are not willing to do. In any case, in the sphere of love, such conflicts do not bode well in the long term for the evolution of the relationship.

When this card is inverted, it indicates that, whether due to lack of capacity, error or ignorance, we will not be able to resolve the conflict that affects us, and may even be embarrassed. Or maybe we're just fed up with the never-ending arguments and decide to give up on such a troubled relationship.

Eight of Wands

DIVINATORY MEANING
Fast advance, high hopes, ambition, hyperactivity. Hasty decisions. Air travel, messages, love letters. Freedom.

INVERTED
Opposition, jealousy, discord, disputes at home. Delay in business or love affairs. Force applied improperly or too hastily will not achieve success. Patience is required.

The Eight of Wands indicates drive and a rapid forward movement, fueled by high hopes. In the context of love, this card suggests a fast and intense courtship, without anything hindering our progress.

If we are alone, the Eight of Wands indicates that we can receive or make ourselves an unexpected proposal or an invitation for a date with someone we are attracted to. This card tells us that we must be open to the opportunities that come our way in love and be ready to act quickly if something of interest arises.

If we are in a relationship, the Eight of Wands indicates that our relationship as a couple could quickly move to the next level, as going on holiday or starting something together. This card suggests that we need to be alert and prepared to act quickly when the opportunity arises.

In general, the Eight of Wands teaches us that we must be open to opportunities that present themselves in our love life and be ready to act quickly when they do. This card indicates a fast and positive movement in love, so it will be convenient for us to be ready to act when the time comes.

If the Eight of Wands is inverted, it indicates conflicts at home, jealousy and arguments. Our love life is hindered and for now it will not be possible to improve it. It is important to take time to consider how we can proceed; although this card suggests haste, acting rashly will not do us any good in this case.

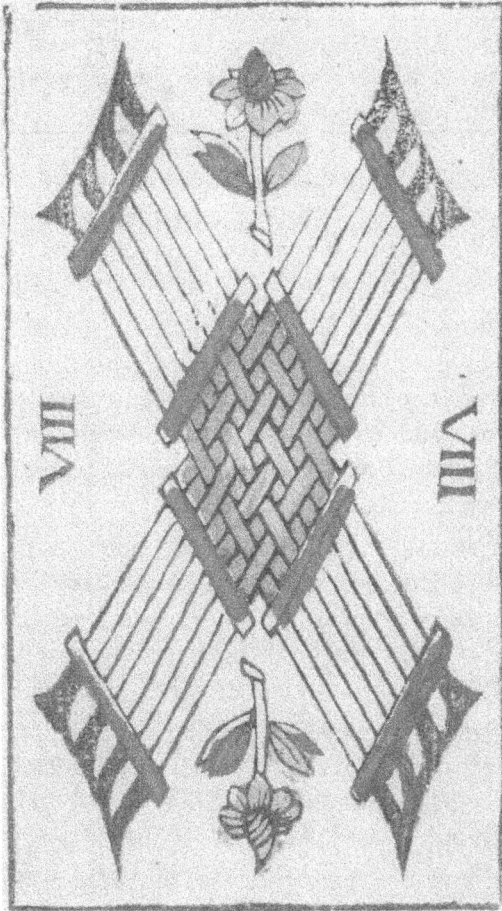

Nine of Wands

DIVINATORY MEANING
Resistance force. Pause in the fight, delays. Victory after overcoming opposition. Health recovery.

INVERTED
Weakness, delays, suspension, adversity, inability to overcome obstacles. Bad health. Patience, prudence and discretion are advised; it is better to stop to avoid complications.

The Nine of Wands is a card that indicates perseverance and resistance, suggesting that we have gone through a troubled period in our relationships, but that we are ready to overcome any obstacle that arises in our love life and social relationships, because we have clear goals.

If we are alone, the Nine of Wands suggests that we have been through a difficult time in love and possibly suffered great disappointment, but that we have overcome adversity and are ready to move on. This card encourages us to stand firm in our convictions and not to give up on finding love. If we have been struggling to find a partner, this card suggests that we keep looking and not give up.

If we are in a relationship, the Nine of Wands tells us that after having overcome certain difficulties, our relationship is stronger than ever. This card urges us to keep our guard up and not allow adversity to discourage us. The Nine of Wands suggests that it is important that we continue to work on our relationship, strengthening it.

In general, the Nine of Wands indicates a period of complications and obstacles in our love and social life, but this card encourages us not to give up and to be persevering in our efforts to find and keep love, and not to give up on our dreams of a satisfying and lasting relationship.

If inverted, the Nine of Wands indicates that we are bowed down by difficulties. Our relationships, in our love or social life, are not going through their best moment, and at this moment we cannot do much to improve them. This card advises us patience, prudence and discretion, if we pressure other people to achieve our desires, we will only achieve counterproductive results.

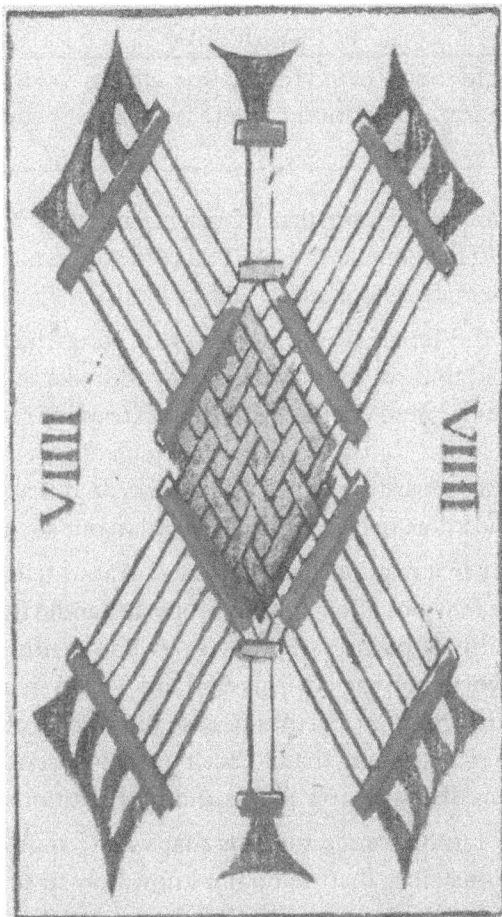

Ten of Wands

DIVINATORY MEANING
Oppression, ordeal. Uncertainty in an enterprise, uncertain efforts, misapplied power, problems that could be solved soon. Feeling overwhelmed, tired, with too many projects or responsibilities.

INVERTED
Failure, possible losses or giving up something to simplify life. Intrigues, separation, emigration. If there is a lawsuit pending there will be losses.

The Ten of Wands is a card that represents a heavy burden or great responsibility. In the context of love, this card suggests that we may be feeling overwhelmed by our social and/or family responsibilities.

If we are alone, the Ten of Wands suggests that we are feeling the weight of loneliness and that we cannot find a way to make our way socially; we find it very difficult to communicate and express our feelings acceptably. It is possible that this is a moment in which other circumstances in our lives, whether regarding to health or work, do not allow us to dedicate the time and effort necessary to get ahead in our social and love life.

If we are already in a relationship, the Ten of Wands tells us that we are overloaded. We may not know how to properly handle the responsibilities that our family or partner imposes on us, and at times we may even wonder if it is worth moving on. This card urges us to share our burdens and seek support from our partner to ease the weight of our responsibilities. If there is something that is causing tension in our relationship, it is important to discuss it as a couple and find solutions together.

In general, the Ten of Wands suggests that we are overloaded or have assumed a responsibility that we do not know how to sustain, which is affecting our relationship life and stressing us a lot. This card urges us to find ways to ease the weight of our obligations and not allow these burdens to overwhelm our relationship. If we work in collaboration with our partner and/or family, looking for solutions together, it will be possible to overcome any obstacle. It is also important that we learn to delegate our responsibilities and not assume all the burden of running a family ourselves.

When inverted, this card indicates a breaking point, the moment when we are forced to recognize that we cannot go ahead with all of our obligations, but must instead renounce some of them. If we don't, our relationships will suffer. It is better to voluntarily give up something, even if it affects our pride, rather than spoil the relationship with our partner or with our family. It may be advisable — if other cards confirm it — to move to a place where we can lead a calmer life, with less stress, or perhaps change jobs or delegate responsibilities. If we can't resolve the issues before we reach the breaking point, a divorce is possible.

Page of Wands

DIVINATORY MEANING
A good foreigner, a messenger or bearer of news. Brilliant, skilful, fiery and daring. Loyal assistant. If it appears next to a card that represents a person, it will give good testimony of him. Evolving creative potential.

INVERTED
Cruel, unstable, superficial, theatrical, arrogant, someone who tries to subjugate you, gossip, slanderous, vindictive. Unable to control his impulses. If you are a woman, it will break your heart. It can be an unfaithful lover, especially with the Seven of Swords. Bad news. Instability.

The Page of Wands is a card that represents youthful energy and enthusiasm. In the context of love, this card suggests that we may be experiencing an exciting new passion or romance in our life. This card also symbolizes a bearer of good news, someone we can trust, and who stimulates us with their passion.

If we are alone, the Page of Wands suggests that there may be someone new in our life or that we are open to new connections and experiences. This card urges us to follow our heart and to dare to take risks in love. A new love can arise spontaneously, and this card encourages us to take the initiative and explore this new relationship.

If we are in a relationship, the Page of Wands suggests that there is a new level of passion and excitement in our current relationship, a renewed interest and energy, which can lead to a greater level of intimacy and emotional connection in our relationship. This card urges us to be creative and adventurous in our love and social relationships, and to explore new ways to connect with our partner. There may also be something new that changes the dynamics of the relationship.

In general, the Page of Wands tells us that we may be experiencing a new passion and excitement in our love life. This card urges us to follow our hearts and take risks in love, as there may be an exciting and meaningful relationship waiting for us.

If it is inverted, the Page of Wands indicates lack of control, an emotional imbalance that can affect our relationships. It can also indicate

that our partner, or a close relationship is trying to manipulate us, it is not sincere or is unfaithful.

Knight of Wands

DIVINATORY MEANING
Departure. Impetuous, passionate and generous protector, but also brutal and unpredictable. Journey into the unknown, opener of new paths, emigration, moving, abandonment, precipitation.

INVERTED
Jealous and conflicting, brutal. Separation, discord, argument, disturbing news. Lack of energy, stagnation. Somebody that only thinks about his desires, without having long-term plans. Give in to temptation.

The Knight of Wands is a card that represents action and passion. In the context of love, this card suggests that we are looking for a fiery and exciting adventure in our love life. If it points to another person, it characterizes a passionate and impetuous man, sometimes excessively, but who has good intentions.

If we are alone, the Knight of Wands suggests that we are ready to embark on a new romantic adventure. This card urges us to be bold and take the initiative. There may be someone in our life that we are drawn to and excited about, and this card encourages us to move on and explore this connection. On the other hand, the Knight of Wands also means great changes and opportunities; a person who comes into our life, and shakes it up, who can be a passionate lover, but is also very impetuous and a bit overbearing.

If we are already in a relationship, this card suggests that a third party may appear in our emotional landscape, someone who changes and shakes up our lives. The Knight of Wands can suddenly turn our lives upside down, possibly for the better, depending on the accompanying cards, motivating us to leave our partner and rethink our lives.

In general, the Knight of Wands indicates that we are looking for an exciting and passionate relationship in our love life. This card encourages us to be daring and not adverse to change, but we must never give up the control of our own life, because the Knight of Wands is so impetuous that they can easily drag us in his wake.

If inverted, this card indicates extreme lack of control, conflict, and emotional imbalance. It can also suggest excesses of all kinds, both in

our treatment of other people, or in the treatment we receive from others. In this case, the Knight of Wands may refer to a jealous, conflictive and selfish person, and they is a temptation that is best avoided. If we are living as a couple, this card can indicate discord or even separation.

Queen of Wands

DIVINATORY MEANING
Kind but strict; energetic and calm; conservative, thrifty and pragmatic. Fruitful in mind and body. A lover of nature and home. She knows how to get what she wants. Speak softly, but carry a big stick. Powerful female figure.

INVERTED
Domineering, intimidating, jealous, dogmatic, arrogant and irrational. Quick to take offense, vindictive. Unfaithful (if the Seven of Swords, The Magician [inverted] or The Hermit [inverted], are next to this card, it would confirm infidelity). Opposition, obstacle, threat.

The Queen of Wands is a card that represents passion, creativity and determination. In the context of love, this card suggests that we are passionate and creative, that we are in control of our love life, although it can also refer to a person with these characteristics that appears in our life. Traditionally, the Queen of Wands depicts a conservative and strict woman who lives in contact with nature, and who, despite her strength of character, is also kind. If for any reason we antagonize her, we will see her intimidating aspect, because she is not someone we can bother with impunity. The Queen of Wands is fruitful, if this card is accompanied by other confirming cards, it may indicate a pregnancy.

If we are alone, the Queen of Wands suggests that we will meet a person with the characteristics described in the previous paragraph. The type of relationship symbolized by this card is not a mere flirtation, but something serious. The Queen of Wands does not waste time on trifles and if we relate to her it is better that we be clear about what life project we want to develop with her.

If we are already in a relationship, the Queen of Wands may be our partner, who is certainly a powerful female figure. If we don't measure up to her, in terms of strength of character, she can subjugate us. But everything she does will be for the benefit of the shared home, the Queen of Wands is a great protector of her family.

In general, the Queen of Wands indicates a solid and pragmatic partner, who supports us, and possibly also pushes us a little. We can trust her,

but we'd better fulfill our responsibilities if we don't want her to take command.

When it is inverted, the Queen of Wands becomes very arrogant and intolerant, and can even be paranoid. She is a woman who is very difficult to live with. If she appears next to some specific cards (see the divinatory meanings above) it would indicate infidelity.

King of Wands

DIVINATORY MEANING
Bold, hasty and generous man. Passionate, strong and proud. A demanding, severe, but well-intentioned boss. He can be a country gentleman, usually married, traditionalist, and fatherly. A good marriage. Entrepreneurial, he knows what he wants and takes care of getting it.

INVERTED
Despotic, severe, dogmatic, arrogant. Intolerant, with excessive and exaggerated ideas. Autocrat, ascetic. He can be cruel.

The King of Wands symbolizes a very passionate and energetic man, with a firm and charismatic personality; he is a born leader, a mature man who can be very protective and loyal to his partner, but also a bit dominant and arrogant in his behavior. This is an individual who is very sure of himself and his feelings, and expects the same from his partner. As usual in court cards, the characteristics just described can apply to the querent as well as to someone who appears in their life.

If we are alone, the King of Wands suggests that this is a good time to seek a relationship with someone with these characteristics, who makes us feel safe and confident. To a woman he would indicate a powerful and protective male figure, who she can trust, and that is a good marriage candidate.

If we are already in a relationship, this card indicates that our relationship is solid and follows the traditional guidelines of mutual support and raising a family. It is a rather comforting than exciting relationship; so that it does not stagnate, it is important to maintain good lines of communication and carry out common projects. On the other hand, also it is important to be aware of any tendencies towards domination or arrogance in our relationship, because, just like his female counterpart (Queen of Wands), if we have a weak personality, the King of Wands can overwhelm us with his protective instinct.

If is inverted, the King of Wands is very dogmatic and excessively strict. He can become a fanatic, following his ideals at any cost and demanding that others abide by the same strict rules that he holds himself to, going so far as to be cruel to impose his view of the world.

ROY·DE·BASTOIIs

Minor Arcana:
Cups

Ace of Cups

DIVINATORY MEANING
Harmony, happiness, pleasure, satisfaction, restoration of health, nutrition, abundance. Your wishes will be fulfilled. Start of a great love. Fertility.

INVERTED
Dissatisfaction. False love, inconstancy, instability, disorders. The end of love, infidelity. Emotional blockage, inability to recognize love or express it. Stagnation. Emotional and/or spiritual lack. Infertility.

The Ace of Cups is associated with the energy of love, creativity, excitement, deep emotional connections, and happiness. It is a very positive card for love and social relationships. Physically it indicates good health and fertility.

If we are alone, this card tells us that we are in a moment in which our emotions flow naturally and we are in harmony with those around us. It can also suggest that a new relationship or love is on the way, and that we will establish a very deep and meaningful emotional connection.

If we are already in a relationship, the Ace of Cups indicates a stage of healing and renewal of the relationship. It can indicate a new beginning, such as a wedding, an engagement, or — if other cards confirm it — the conception of a child.

In general, the Ace of Cups suggests that we should be open to new emotional experiences and allow our feelings to guide our love decisions. This card can also be a call to reflection, so that we remain well in tune with our most intimate desires and let our feelings flow. To find happiness in love we must be able to listen to our inner voice.

If the Ace of Cups is inverted, it tells us that we are emotionally blocked and do not allow ourselves the free expression of our emotions. It also indicates a low emotional intelligence, a spiritual deficiency that we must overcome if we want to enjoy a harmonious and happy life. Physically, it can indicate infertility.

Two of Cups

DIVINATORY MEANING
Love, harmony, warm friendship, cooperation. Close relationship with a soul mate. Good card for business and love.

INVERTED
Disagreements, opposition, false or unsatisfactory love, disappointment, misunderstanding, carelessness, debauchery, dissipation, jealousy. Crisis in a couple relationship.

The Two of Cups indicates a period of great harmony with like-minded people, when we can cultivate close love and friendship relationships with other people, or even establish close business partnerships. This card represents union, harmony and cooperation in our relationships.

If we are alone, the Two of Cups offers us the encouraging message that a new love relationship is on the horizon. It can be a sign that we will soon meet someone with whom we will have a very special connection. If we have already met someone, this card suggests that the relationship may be in a very sweet and harmonious moment and that it will be possible to take it to the next level.

If we are already in a relationship, the Two of Cups indicates that we have a deep emotional and affective connection with our partner. This card suggests that the relationship is in a stage of harmony and is becoming stronger, reaching greater intimacy and commitment.

In general, the Two of Cups is a very positive card when it comes to love and relationships. It suggests that the emotional connection between two people is strong and authentic, and that there is great opportunity for growth and evolution in the relationship.

If it is inverted, the Two of Cups suggests a crisis in the relationship, caused by misunderstandings, jealousy, and perhaps infidelity. Depending on the neighboring cards, this card will only indicate a stage, which we can overcome, or the end of the relationship.

Three of Cups

DIVINATORY MEANING
Abundance. Joy, hospitality, success. Sharing the good things of life. Procreation, adoption. Happy result.

INVERTED
Excesses in eating, drinking or sensuality. Unbridled passion. Sex without love. Discord or estrangement between friends. A close alliance between two people rules out a third party. Problems in parent-child relationships.

The Three of Cups represents celebration, friendship, and emotional connection with our loved ones. In love, this card can signify a happy and satisfying relationship where the parties feel emotionally connected. It can indicate a happy celebration or event in the relationship, such as an engagement, anniversary, or even a wedding.

If we are not yet in a relationship, the Three of Cups suggests that in an upcoming meeting with friends we may meet someone special or have an emotional connection with someone with whom we will share common interests and hobbies.

If we are already in a relationship, the Three of Cups indicates that this is a time of celebration, when we share the good things in life, both with our partner and with a circle of like-minded friends. The plans we have will come to fruition successfully. This card can also indicate procreation or adoption, if confirmed by neighboring cards.

In general, the Three of Cups is very positive for love and friendship; teaches us that love is a source of happiness and that it is important to share it with others, so that it can multiply.

If it is inverted, this card tells us that excesses can damage our relationships with those close to us. It can also indicate infidelity or debauchery, a tendency to live only in the now, without worrying about the long-term consequences of our acts. If other cards confirm this, it may suggest that we are being left behind by two people who are ganging up against us.

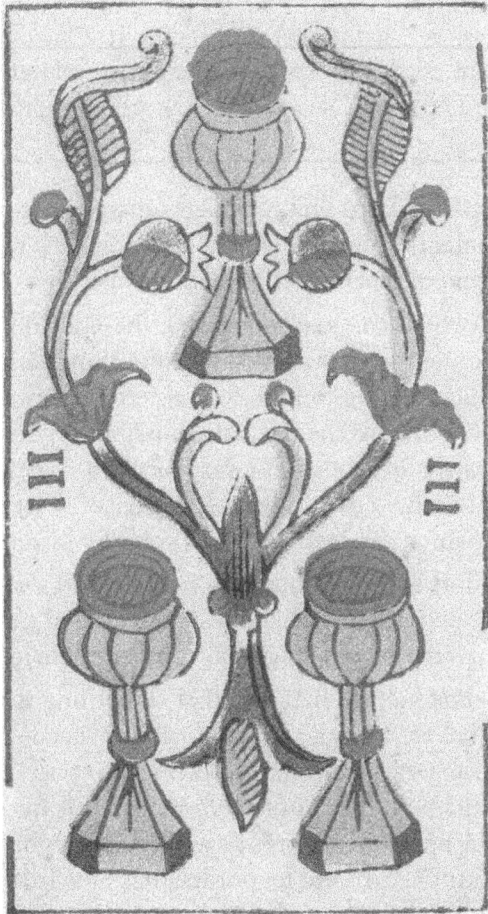

Four of Cups

DIVINATORY MEANING
Boredom, reluctance, indolence, wearisomeness. Stationary period of life. Kindness of others. Rejection or inability to see opportunities. Isolation, extreme introversion.

INVERTED
Awakening from a period of dissatisfaction or contemplation. New relationships are possible. New goals, new ambition, new knowledge. Omen.

The Four of Cups is a card that represents dissatisfaction, apathy, and emotional discontent. In love, this card can indicate a moment of stagnation or boredom, of disconnection with the world.

If we are alone (which this card suggests), the Four of Cups indicates a period of discontent with our lives, when nothing satisfies us and we don't even feel like moving to look for something new; in fact we feel bored and possibly discard the romantic possibilities that are presented to us, or perhaps we are not even aware of them. We may have a tendency to compare others to an idealized image of what we are looking for in a partner, which can lead us to feel perpetually dissatisfied.

If we make an effort and open our eyes to the world around us, we will see that there are people who are interested in us, and that we must take the first step to overcome our stagnation and extreme introspection.

If we are with someone, we may feel that something is missing in our relationship or that we are not receiving what we need emotionally. We may also have exaggerated aspirations, which our partner will never be able to fulfil, which will harm our relationship. It is important that we wake up from the apathy that grips us and establish good communication links with our partner and let our feelings flow freely.

In general, the Four of Cups suggests that it is important to pay attention to our emotional needs and make the necessary changes in our love life in order to find the happiness and fulfillment we seek. But we must be realistic, if we look for perfection we will never find it; let's accept what life offers us and do not close ourselves off, we must learn to share the blessings we have with others and also be willing to accept what they offer us.

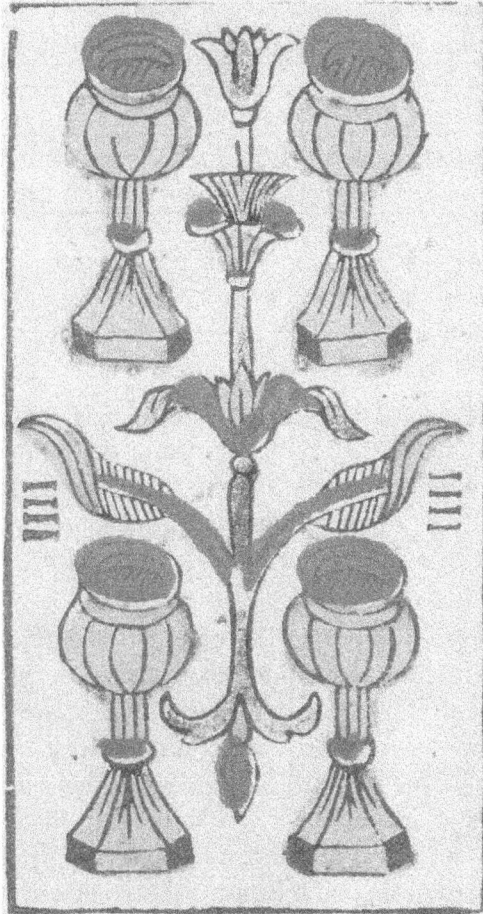

If the Four of Cups is inverted, it indicates that we are coming out of an emotionally unsatisfactory period. When we open our eyes, we will see that we have many possibilities to establish new relationships. It is possible that some unexpected event wakes us up and excites us, making us decide to participate in social life or become interested in new opportunities that now we can see.

Five of Cups

DIVINATORY MEANING
Disappointment, loss, disappointment, unexpected misfortune, false projects, imperfection. Mourning, lament. Breakup of a relationship, union without love, with bitterness and frustration. Betrayal from a loved one. Regrets, difficulty in overcoming the past.

INVERTED
New happiness. Return of an old love or a friend. Alliance. New hopes, new perspectives after overcoming a period of mourning or regret.

The Five of Cups is associated with sadness, loss and grief. In love, it can indicate mourning for the loss of a person, regret for the mistakes made that led us to lose someone, or disappointment or disillusionment with someone with whom we were or are intimately linked.

If we are alone, this card teaches us that as long as we do not overcome the regret for a failed past relationship, and we begin to look to the future, and not to the past, we will not be able to be happy. Although it seems to us that we cannot be happy without someone we lost, that is not so; we must be aware of our blessings and learn to be happy with what we have.

If we are in a relationship, the Five of Cups can indicate a feeling of dissatisfaction and discouragement, that our relationship fills us with bitterness and frustration. Perhaps we no longer have expectations of being able to improve our relationship and we don't know what to do, and that is why we are discouraged. Likewise, this card indicates that to get ahead in a relationship we have to learn to forgive, if we do not overcome the past we will not have a future either. In some cases, the Five of Cups can indicate that it is time to let go of a relationship that is no longer healthy and fulfilling (if other cards confirm this); although it can be painful, sometimes it is necessary to give up something in order to move forward and find better opportunities in the future.

In general, the Five of Cups is a card that indicates the need to face and overcome negative emotions and challenges in love. In time, we may find that sadness and disappointment are temporary and we may be able to find hope and happiness again, either by improving an existing relationship, or by seeking a new one.

If this card is inverted, it means that we will overcome our resentment and bitterness for past sorrows. Perhaps an old love or friend will return, or we may meet a new person, allowing us to put past hardships behind us for good.

Six of Cups

DIVINATORY MEANING
Influences from the past, love, memories; friendship, happiness or opportunity that comes from the past. Inheritance. Money through marriage or partners.

INVERTED
Living too much in the past. Associates or friends who are worthless. Uncertain plans or expectations, inability to adapt to changes. Bad habits that we drag from the past.

The Six of Cups is related to nostalgia and memories of the past. As for love, this card can indicate that we are remembering an old love or that a friendship or love from the past reappears in our lives.

If we are alone, this card may indicate that we are looking for a relationship that gives us comfort and security, like we experienced in the past, or that we want to reconnect with someone from our past. In any case, it is important that we reflect on our true feelings and that we do not idealize the past too much, but we must also be alert not to miss any opportunity for love that comes from the past. The Six of Cups can also indicate the need to heal old emotional wounds before moving forward in a new relationship.

If we are already in a relationship, this card suggests a period of nostalgia, perhaps we are not completely satisfied with our current life, and we look back with longing for the past. The Six of Cups can also indicate that a person we met in the past is influencing our lives again, or that we can benefit from associating with them.

In general, the Six of Cups indicates that a person or influence from the past is going to affect our present in a positive way. We may also meet a person who is linked in some way to our past.

If it is inverted, the Six of Cups warns us against allowing memories and nostalgia for the past to prevent us from looking forward. It is good to remember the past, but we must live for the future. In the social and loving sphere, idealizing our past loves will not help us at all, but, on the contrary, it will harm us, preventing us from adapting to the present. This card also suggests that we are being harmed by old friends or a

lover that no longer bring us anything good; if we want to be happy and get ahead it would be better to forget them.

Seven of Cups

DIVINATORY MEANING
Illusory dreams, foolish expectations, disappointment, broken promises. Intoxication, corruption. Passivity, no action is taken to make our fantasies real.

INVERTED
Determination, desire, project, intelligent choice. Open your eyes, recover your common sense.

The Seven of Cups is related with illusory dreams, fantasy, and the imagination. In love, this arcane can indicate that we are in a state of confusion, indecision or lack of clarity regarding our feelings or those of our partner, or that perhaps we dream of loving a certain person, but we do not dare to take the first step.

If we are alone, the Seven of Cups can indicate the presence of illusions or fantasies that do not correspond to the reality of the relationship we have with a certain person, which can lead to disappointment or disappointment in the future. It can also suggest that we are considering various options or possibilities in the realm of love, but that we have not yet made a clear decision, or that perhaps we are unable to overcome the fantasizing stage to express our feelings openly.

If we are in a relationship, the Seven of Cups teaches us that it is convenient for us to be realistic and honest with ourselves when it comes to our feelings and expectations concerning our partner. It also indicates that the communication channels with our partner are not working well, or that one of the members of the relationship is trying to deceive the other.

In general, this card invites us to reflection and internal exploration in order to make informed and conscious decisions in love. It is important that we overcome our indecision and leave dreams behind, to act in the real world.

If it is inverted, this card is more positive; it tells us that we will overcome illusory dreams and passivity, making a determination and facing new vital projects. In the realm of love, this means that we will take concrete steps and express our feelings openly to the person we care about.

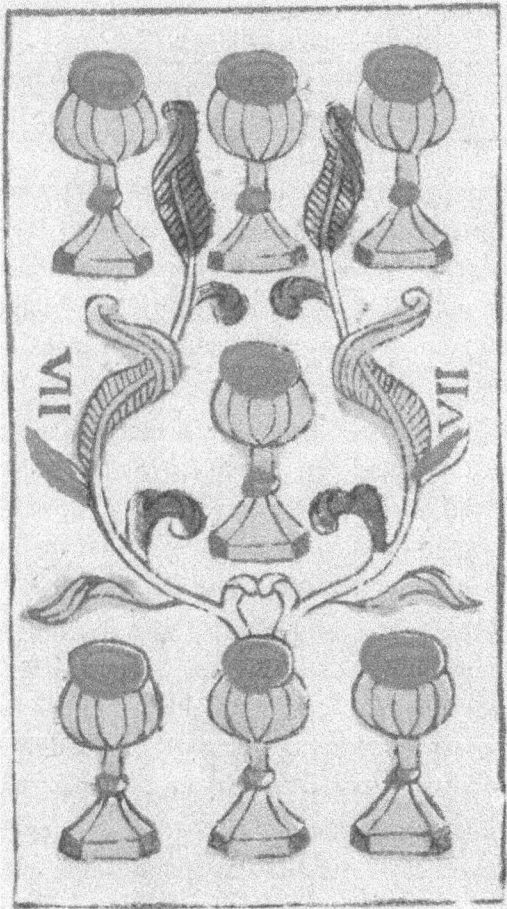

Eight of Cups

Divinatory Meaning
Instability. Success or abandoned relationship, perhaps in pursuit of something higher. Wandering. Love disappointment, changes in the family.

Inverted
Joy, happiness. A new love or a new interest in material things, causing us to defer our spiritual interests.

The Eight of Cups can represent the search for a deeper or more meaningful love experience, or indicate that we are dissatisfied with superficial relationships and are looking for something more authentic and true. It can also indicate a period in which we privilege the spiritual world over the material things and decide to distance ourselves from our relationships.

If we are alone, the Eight of Cups indicates that we are recovering from a heartbreak and our situation is unstable. We still haven't decided what we want to do with our live and we are looking for new options. This card can also refer to the step young people take when they leave the family home, in search of new opportunities.

If we are in a relationship, the Eight of Cups can indicate that we are feeling emotionally overwhelmed and need to get away to recover and find a new perspective. This can mean either taking a break from our love relationships, or breaking up for good (depending on the neighboring cards) to focus on ourselves and our personal growth.

In general, the Eight of Cups suggests that we need to make a significant change in the area of love and our relationships, either in order to search for something different or to take the time we need to clear our minds and grow spiritually. This card can indicate a physical separation from our family or partner, or simply refer to a stage in our life in which we do not put them first, but instead focus on our spiritual growth.

When inverted, this card indicates the opposite. We can expect a new love or new relationships that will fill us with happiness and enthusiasm.

Nine of Cups

DIVINATORY MEANING
You will get what you want. Victory. Physical and emotional well-being. Happiness, concord, contentment.

INVERTED
Dissatisfaction. Errors, complacency, vanity, insecurity, losses, disputes, imperfections, excesses of food and/or drink, excessive indulgence. You won't get what you want.

The Nine of Cups is also known as the Wish Card, and is often associated with personal satisfaction and the fulfillment of our wishes. In love, this card suggests the possibility of finding happiness and fulfillment in a relationship.

If we are alone, this card suggests that soon we will have the opportunity to meet someone who meets our expectations and makes us feel happy and satisfied, or if we already know someone, our wishes will come true. It also indicates a period of physical well-being and emotional clarity, when we know what we want and how to get it.

If we already have a partner, this card indicates that we are experiencing a stage of harmony and satisfaction with our partner, and that we have a solid and lasting relationship.

In general, the Nine of Cups suggests that it is important to maintain a positive and grateful attitude towards love and relationships in our lives. If we have experienced difficulties in the past, this card invites us to trust ourselves and to continue working to make our desires and aspirations in love come true.

When it is inverted, this card indicates that we will not get what we are looking for. Concerning love, conflicts and disputes will not allow us to enjoy harmonious relationships with our partner or with our loved ones. The Nine of Cups also warns us against excesses of all kinds, which can damage both our physical and emotional health as well as our social life.

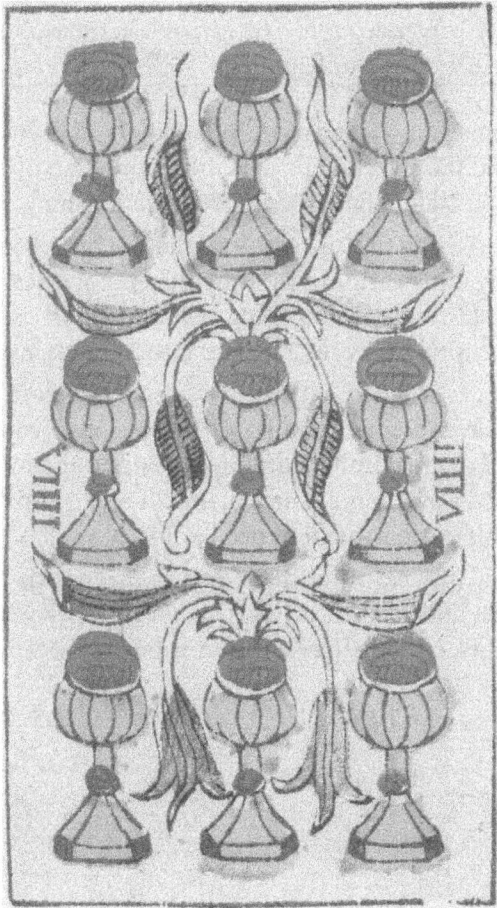

Ten of Cups

DIVINATORY MEANING
Perfect well-being and love, enduring success, peace at home, great friendship, harmony. Predominance of spiritual values.

INVERTED
Serious dispute, violence, domestic quarrel, betrayal, loss of a friendship. Debauchery, abuse, unhappiness.

The Ten of Cups is associated with happiness and emotional fulfillment in love and family. It represents the completion of a cycle and the achievement of a stable, happy, and deep relationship.

If we are alone, the Ten of Cups suggests that we have good prospects of starting a family. This card can indicate the end of a search period and the arrival of a lasting and satisfying relationship. It can also indicate that a relationship we have will evolve into a happy and harmonious union.

If we already have our own family or partner, this card indicates an excellent period of great understanding, harmony and love. If any problem arises, we can overcome it and maintain a harmonious and happy relationship with our partner and our family.

If it is inverted, this card indicates disturbances with our partner. It warns us against abuse or infidelity that can ruin peace at home. It can also refer to fights, or the betrayal of a member of the family or a friend.

Page of Cups

DIVINATORY MEANING
Calm and studious; gentle, kind and dreamy. Good omen, news or proposal, perhaps of marriage, or the birth of a child. Uncertain beginning of a relationship, attempt to clarify one's feelings.

INVERTED
Seductive, dilettante, not very serious, useless and indolent. Unpleasant news, happiness is elusive. Flattery, deceit, artifice.

The Page of Cups is related to youth, sensitivity, creativity and emotions. In love, it can indicate the emergence of a new relationship or a crush in the making. This card suggests that we are willing to express our feelings and let ourselves be carried away by our emotions, however, it can also be indicative of a somewhat immature or insecure attitude in love. The pages generally indicate young people, who are starting out in life, this particular page refers to someone sensitive, kind, who wants to start a romantic relationship.

If we are alone, this card can indicate a new love that comes into our life, or a news or proposal (even of marriage), that we can make or receive. It also tells us that we are open to love and we will get it.

If the Page of Cups appears in a reading related to an existing relationship, it may indicate that we need to communicate and express our feelings better, so that the relationship continues to grow and strengthen. It is possible that we are looking for a deeper and more authentic emotional connection with our partner, or it can also indicate an energy of romanticism and creativity that we are experiencing in our current relationship, which can lead to moments of intimacy and deep emotional connection. It also may mean good news, as the birth of a child.

In general, the Page of Cups is a positive card in love and suggests that we should be open to our emotions and new opportunities that arise in our social life. This card always suggests openness to love, the possibility of new relationships, and an emotional approach to love life.

When it is inverted, this card can also suggest love relationships, but in this case we are in danger of being deceived, or perhaps someone will flatter us to take advantage of us. Also, the Page of Cups, inverted, can

VALET·DE·COVPES

indicate a relationship with a lazy playboy, who is neither serious nor sincere and is reckless.

Knight of Cups

DIVINATORY MEANING
Arrival of a young man, perhaps an artist, sincere and open, attractive and romantic, a lazy but well-intentioned dreamer of sensual pleasures. It can mean a messenger, a proposal or an invitation. Attraction, opportunity.

INVERTED
Fraud, betrayal, deceit. Devious and cunning, lazy, sensual. A Don Juan. Arrival of an anonymous, breach of trust, double game.

The Knight of Cups is related to emotion and love at its best. This card represents a handsome young man who moves with grace and elegance, always seeking the fulfillment of his deepest dreams and desires. The Knight of Cups indicates a romantic approach, in which love and passion are the main engines. This card suggests the appearance of a sensitive, creative, affectionate and passionate man, who can be a great sentimental partner.

The Knight of Cups suggests that we are in a stage of emotional openness, ready to explore new romantic possibilities. This card invites us to connect with our deepest feelings and to let our intuition and heart guide us towards love. In the external aspect, it can also indicate the arrival of a new love in our life, which attracts us a lot, and whose main ingredients will be sensitivity and passion. Someone offers us an attractive opportunity, are we going to accept it?

When inverted, this card warns us against a Don Juan who tries to seduce us, someone who can play with our feelings to take advantage of us without giving us anything in return. He may try to manipulate us, either by flattering, threatening, or even blackmailing us. This is not a propitious time to blindly trust anyone, let's keep our guard up.

CAVALLIER·DE·COVPE

Queen of Cups

DIVINATORY MEANING
Dreamy, calm, poetic, imaginative, kind, but not willing to go to much trouble to help another. Loyal, devoted, loving wife and/or mother. Apothecary, herbalist, pharmacist. Gift of vision, fortune teller, keeper of secrets. Happiness and pleasure.

INVERTED
Dishonest, immoral and vicious woman. Seductive heartbreaker, manipulative. Untrustworthy. Closing in on oneself, distrust, hiding one's own emotions; hostility, rejection of emotional contacts.

The Queen of Cups represents love, intuition, empathy and sensitivity. In the field of love, this card can indicate a stable and deep relationship, based on trust and mutual respect. The Queen of Cups is an emotionally mature person who knows how to handle her feelings effectively, making her a caring and understanding partner.

If we are alone, the Queen of Cups suggests that we might be looking for a deep and meaningful connection with someone who is emotionally receptive and understanding. The Queen of Cups can also indicate that we will soon meet someone who will be a great emotional support in our life. It can also be a sign for us to listen to our intuition in love relationships, as this card suggests that our instincts and feelings are wise and trustworthy.

If we are already in a relationship, the Queen of Cups tells us that this is a time when we need to open up emotionally to our partner and express our deepest feelings. In general, the Queen of Cups is a card that indicates love, compassion, and emotional support in relationships.

In general, the Queen of Cups indicates that we are in a time of great emotional sensitivity and understanding, and that we need to pay attention to our feelings and emotional needs, connecting with our deepest self. Externally, it is a period to be more sympathetic to our relationships.

If it is inverted, the Queen of Cups can indicate that we are dealing with confused feelings and intense emotions that may be negatively affecting our love relationships. We are isolating ourselves from others and letting mistrust ruin our social relationships; let's not hide our emotions.

Externally, the Queen of Cups can indicate a seductress, completely un-trustworthy, who tries to manipulate us.

King of Cups

DIVINATORY MEANING
A man familiar with science, art, religion, or philosophy. Doctor, psychologist, teacher, man of God. A good friend, liberal, idealistic and creative. Friendly and willing to take some responsibility or provide help. Head of household. Emotional maturity.

INVERTED
Evil and ruthless. Untrustworthy, lying and vicious. Double game. Beware of deceptions. Inability to overcome past traumas, negative world view.

The King of Cups suggests emotional maturity and deep, sincere feelings. In love, this can indicate a stable relationship, full of affection and emotional commitment. This card is also associated with understanding and empathy, suggesting that in a relationship, both parties can communicate effectively and understand each other's needs. Additionally, the King of Cups is related with intuition and emotional intelligence, and can symbolize a person who is emotionally supportive and understanding. In general, the King of Cups suggests an emotionally satisfying and balanced relationship.

If we are looking for a partner, the King of Cups can be a sign that we should look for someone who has the characteristics described in the previous paragraph, since he is likely to be a loving and understanding partner. The King of Cups is the archetype of the mature man with great emotional intelligence. When it comes to love, this archetype suggests that a person who has this energy is a good listener, compassionate, and empathetic. He is also able to understand and express his emotions clearly and effectively.

If we already are in a relationship, the King of Cups can indicate that our relationship is emotionally satisfying and balanced, and that both members respect and support each other.

If inverted, the King of Cups symbolizes someone who deceives us and only seeks to take advantage of us. On the internal side, it suggests that we have an emotional blockage caused by past traumas, and as long as we don't overcome it, we will continue to have problems relating to oth-

ers, due to excessive mistrust, which will adversely affect our social and
loving relationships.

Minor Arcana: Coins[1]

---

1   Coins are called Pentacles in the RWS Tarot, Disks in the Thot Tarot.

Ace of Coins

DIVINATORY MEANING
Money works for you. The beginning of prosperity and wealth. Achievements, success. Perfect satisfaction. Security, material well-being.

INVERTED
Money dominates you. Problems with money, insecurity. Prosperity without happiness, money corrupts. Avarice. Ostentation.

The Ace of Coins is often associated with security and stable emotional relationships. This card predicts success, fortune and prosperity, both in life in general, as well as in our love life and interpersonal relationships. It indicates consolidation, which means that the relationships we have will bear fruit, and because it promises achievements, it is a good time to start new relationships.

If we are alone, the Ace of Coins indicates that our life is stable and we are progressing. Although it is not a card that specifically points to social relationships or love, the Ace of Pentacles can indicate the beginning of a new emotionally satisfying relationship, because we have the necessary foundation to develop satisfying and happy relationships with other people, both in the field of friendship and love.

If we are in a relationship, the Ace of Coins indicates stability and satisfaction. This is a good time to share the good things in life with our partner and make plans for the future.

In general, the Ace of Coins is a very positive card that suggests that we are at a stage in our lives in which we can achieve great emotional, financial and spiritual stability, which can translate into true and lasting love.

When it is inverted, in relation to love, the Ace of Coins indicates that we try to pretend what we are not, due to our insecurity that we try to hide behind a façade of well-being. We should not trust unknown people, let's be prudent when establishing new relationships.

Two of Coins

DIVINATORY MEANING
Ups and downs of luck and/or mood. Alternation of profit and loss. Balance in the middle of change. Ability to adapt to new circumstances. Some complications. Ambivalence, going forward and backward.

INVERTED
Lack of safety. Difficulty adapting to new circumstances. Inability to bring projects to a successful conclusion.

The Two of Coins indicates an ambivalent situation, where nothing is certain, even if we maintain our balance in the midst of change. It can also suggest insecurity and indecision, we don't know whether to move forward or go back.

If we are alone, the Two of Coins suggest that we are in a period of many changes, and perhaps this is not the best time to establish a permanent relationship. However, this card also tells us that we have the necessary versatility to establish relationships, which, albeit transitory, may be satisfying; it even suggests that we can manage several relationships simultaneously.

If we are in a relationship, this card can indicate that there is good communication and a balanced distribution of responsibilities with our partner, although the relationship is not stable, but rather it is evolving and some complications may arise. On the other hand, the Two of Coins can also indicate the need to make adjustments and changes in our relationship to maintain balance. There may be aspects that need to be reconsidered or renegotiated to avoid imbalances that could put our relationship at risk.

The Two of Coins does not tell us where our relationship is headed, the ambivalence that characterizes it may well indicate a relationship that is not going anywhere, as well as refer to a relationship that is developing. In any case, the neighboring cards will help us clarify the matter.

In general, the Two of Coins is a card that speaks of adaptation and flexibility in our life and love relationships, and of the importance of maintaining good balance between giving and receiving, so that relationships are satisfactory, in the midst of a changing situation.

If it is inverted, this card indicates that we are stressed by the complications and uncertainty of this period. If we are already in a relationship,
we may not know how to make the necessary adjustments to adapt to
the changing situation in which we find ourselves, which can harm our
relationship. If we are alone, it will be very difficult for us to establish
loving relationships, because we are too rigid and it is very difficult for
us to adapt to changes and novelties.

Three of Coins

DIVINATORY MEANING
Job well done, mastery. Material progress, business transactions. Prestigious member of a brotherhood.

INVERTED
Incapable and irresponsible. Insufficient skill or knowledge to achieve what is intended. Futile efforts, stubborn, unable to learn from their mistakes. More concern for profit than for the quality of work. It is similar to the Eight of Coins inverted in terms of poor work, but in this case it indicates incompetency rather than cheating. Decrease in wealth, rank and social status.

The Three of Coins often is associated with teamwork and collaboration with others. In love, this card can indicate a period of cooperation and harmony within a relationship.

If we are alone, we may find someone with whom we can work as a team and create a strong and lasting connection. It can also be a time when we are seriously considering committing to someone, perhaps starting to build a life together. The Three of Coins suggests that any effort we make to carry out a life project with another person will be worthwhile, since the fruits of our collaboration will be lasting and rewarding.

If we are in a relationship, the Three of Coins emphasizes the importance of communication and planning to keep our relationship healthy and balanced. Also, this card can suggest that it is a good time to get involved in creative activities or shared projects with our partner. It also indicates that we have a prominent position within the family.

In general, this card suggests a solid and harmonious relationship in which collaboration with our partner is valued to carry out common plans. Also this is a good time to cultivate new loving relationships with people from our same field of activity.

If it is inverted, this card indicates that one of the members of a couple is unable to maintain a healthy relationship, due to their lack of seriousness and responsibility; neighboring cards can clarify whether this refers to us or our partner. If we want to form a new relationship, this is not a good time, because we will not be able to do it.

Four of Coins

DIVINATORY MEANING
Control and structure. Power. Material gain and security. A gift or an inheritance. Greed, materialism. To some extent it is similar to the 9 of Coins with the pair control/loss control and inheritance.

INVERTED
Lack of control, lack of structure. Limitation, obstacles, material setback, losses, uncertainty and delay, waste.

The Four of Coins is often interpreted as a card of material and emotional attachment, rather than pure, selfless love. This card suggests that we are jealous and possessive in our relationships. It also indicates reluctance to change.

If we are alone, the Four of Coins indicates that we are too attached to certain ideas about what a relationship should be, or that we are afraid of leaving our comfort zone to search for something more meaningful. We may need to work on our self-esteem and our ability to trust others in order to find a satisfying and healthy love relationship. However, this card also tells us that we can receive a pleasant surprise, someone is interested in us and we have the possibility of establishing a satisfactory relationship.

If we are not alone, the Four of Coins indicates stability, and dedication to our relationship or family; we are protective and take every possible precaution to keep our relationship safe from any dangers. We must be careful not to exaggerate our care and precautions, which can become too restrictive.

In general, the Four of Coins suggests that it is important to find a balance between material security and free emotional expression in love relationships. We may need to put aside our fears and worries a bit in order to open up to a deeper and more meaningful relationship.

When it is inverted, the Four of Coins indicates that, if we have a relationship, it is characterized by lack of control and excesses, perhaps we do not know how to set limits to our partner, or it may be that we ourselves are the ones who lack all restraint, that is to say that there are excesses that prevent us from keeping our relationship balanced. If we are alone, this card, inverted, indicates obstacles and limitations.

Five of Coins

Divinatory Meaning
Poverty, indigence, hardship, insecurity, loss of money or employment. Good luck in love, lovers, love or friendship in the middle of trouble.

Inverted
New job or opportunity. Productive work. Bad luck in love.

The Five of Coins is generally associated with financial hardship and lack of structure in our live, but in love it means lovers. It promises us good luck in love.

If we are alone, this card tells us that although we are going through a time of financial hardship and insecurity, we will find someone to love, who will give us comfort.

If we are in a relationship, the Five of Coins can indicate that financial or material difficulties are affecting our relationship. This is a good time to get closer to our partner and share the feelings of our heart. Although, for the moment, the outside world appears hostile, we can always rejoice and lean on the love of our loved ones. Nor can we forget the literal meaning of this card: lovers; in other words, the Five of Coins suggests that we can establish a relationship with someone else, who offers us emotional support.

In general, the Five of Coins is related to difficulties and lack of material resources, but emotionally, it indicates that we can enjoy a close relationship with someone who will offer us comfort.

In case of being inverted, the Five of Coins poses an exactly reversed scenario. We will have bad luck in love, but we will prosper materially.

Six of Coins

DIVINATORY MEANING
Prosper and share your blessings with others. Balance of income and expenses. Gifts, salary increase. Transitory situation.

INVERTED
Proud of his wealth, spendthrift, charity for self-aggrandizement. Offering a bribe, envy, jealousy, bad debt.

The Six of Coins represents generosity and good balance in relationships. In love, this card can indicate a relationship in which both parties freely share their emotions and possessions, it is a relationship based on collaboration and mutual support.

If we are alone, the Six of Coins promises us that we will go through a period of intense social relationships, marked by good balance. Since one of its meanings is gift, it is possible that we receive favors from a person. It also indicates that we are looking for a relationship in which there is reciprocity of giving and receiving, or that we are being generous with others and that this attitude is valued and appreciated by the people with whom we relate.

If we are already with someone, this card indicates an excellent balance, a relationship in which both parties communicate and help each other lovingly.

In general, the Six of Coins indicates that we must balance what we give and what we receive, it is good to be generous with others, but we must not let others abuse us, without offering anything in return. Also this card tells us is that although in interpersonal relationships, everything is a game of give and take, we must be generous and accept that not all our good deeds will be reciprocated by others.

If the card is inverted, it is a sign of jealousy, of wanting to monopolize someone's favors or pretending to receive something without offering anything in return. It also indicates a pretentious attitude, that is, pretending that we have qualities that in reality we do not possess.

Seven of Coins

DIVINATORY MEANING
Disappointment, money worries, greed, anxiety, excessive claims, reckless speculation, loss of money, unpaid loan, miserable result, delay.

INVERTED
Delayed success after hard work. Work done for the love of work, but without expecting material rewards.

The Seven of Coins suggests the need to reflect and be patient when it comes to love and personal relationships. It can indicate that we are taking some time to evaluate our options and consider which path we should follow in our relationships. We may feel that we have been investing too much in a relationship and have not yet seen the expected results, so it may be necessary to evaluate if it is worth moving on or if it is better to leave that relationship behind, but we must not be impatient or despair, let's not be too quick to write anyone off.

If we are alone, the Seven of Coins is a sign that we should be patient and keep working on our relationships, even if we don't get results in the short term.

If we are already in a relationship, the Seven of Coins can indicate that the relationship is in an evaluation stage, in which both partners are reflecting on what they have invested in the relationship and wondering if they are getting what they expect. It may be a time to be patient and see if the efforts put into the relationship will pay off in the long run. This card can also suggest the need to make adjustments and changes in the relationship to make it more fulfilling and valuable.

If it is inverted, the Seven of Coins has a similar meaning, what changes are our feelings; when the card appears upright it indicates concern and doubt, because immediate results are not obtained, inverted, immediate results are not obtained either, but that does not cause us anxiety. In this case, we do what seems best to us without worrying about obtaining short-term results, because we know that, in the long run, everything balances in life.

Eight of Coins

DIVINATORY MEANING
Prudence, dedication, routinary and patient progress. The first step in a profitable profession. Learning a business or profession. Skill in material matters. Health, balance, stability.

INVERTED
Seeking immediate gains without worrying about long-term results. Attention to appearances and neglect of important things. Vanity, greed, fraud, extortion, usury, hypocrisy. Impatience, dissatisfaction with current circumstances. Similar to the inverted 3 of Coins, but much more negative.

The Eight of Coins is related to work, dedication and the ability to perfect ourselves in a profession. As for love, it can indicate that we are focusing on our career or improving our skills in some field, which can lead to our social and love life being affected or postponed, but this card can also refer to a relationship that is developing slowly, that we are developing step by step.

If we are alone, this card may indicate that it is a good time to focus on ourselves and our personal development before seeking a serious relationship. However, it can also refer to a relationship that progresses slowly, but non-stop, without great fanfare, but earnestly.

If we are already in a relationship, the Eight of Coins urges us to take care of all the little details that help make a relationship grow and perdure. More than grand gestures, this card tells us to take care of the little things in everyday life, showing kindness and consideration to our partner, and giving they the attention they deserve.

In general, the Eight of Coins suggests a focus on personal and professional growth, which can influence our love life, but only in the long term. This card also teaches us that we must take constant care of our relationships, so that they flourish and last. In short, let's take care of ourselves, but let's not neglect our relationships.

When inverted, this card indicates that we must be careful of someone who wants to take advantage of us, feigning feelings that are not real, a person who only knows how to take, but not give. It also teaches us to be patient and not to take shortcuts in love, let's not cheat, let's be honest.

Nine of Coins

DIVINATORY MEANING
Achievements, prudence, stability, self-discipline, independence. Practical wisdom limited to one's own domain. Solitary enjoyment of the good things in life. Inheritance (if other cards confirm it).

INVERTED
Disappointment. Material losses or a friendship. Project canceled. Theft, cheating, carelessness.

The Nine of Coins is often interpreted as a card of stability and material achievements, which can indicate independence and self-sufficiency in love, meaning that we are capable of taking care of ourselves and do not need to depend on another person to feel complete.

If we are alone, the Nine of Coins suggests that we are enjoying life and being successful in our career and/or finances, which in turn may attract someone who values those qualities. It can also be a reminder to try to open up a little more to the world, to get out of our comfort zone, to enjoy life more fully and share it with someone.

If we are already in a relationship, the Nine of Coins can suggest that we are enjoying a stable relationship in which we feel safe and comfortable. However, we must not fall into a routinary life or postpone our relationship to a second place, nor neglect our social life. It can also indicate a couple with little social life, who live in their own world.

In general, the Nine of Coins indicates stability and a calm life, circumscribed to the area in which we feel safe. In love, it indicates a stable and harmonious relationship, but if we are alone, this card it is not a very promising omen for love.

If it is inverted, the Nine of Coins warns us against deceit and people who try to take advantage of our good faith. A love relationship may end or a friend may move away.

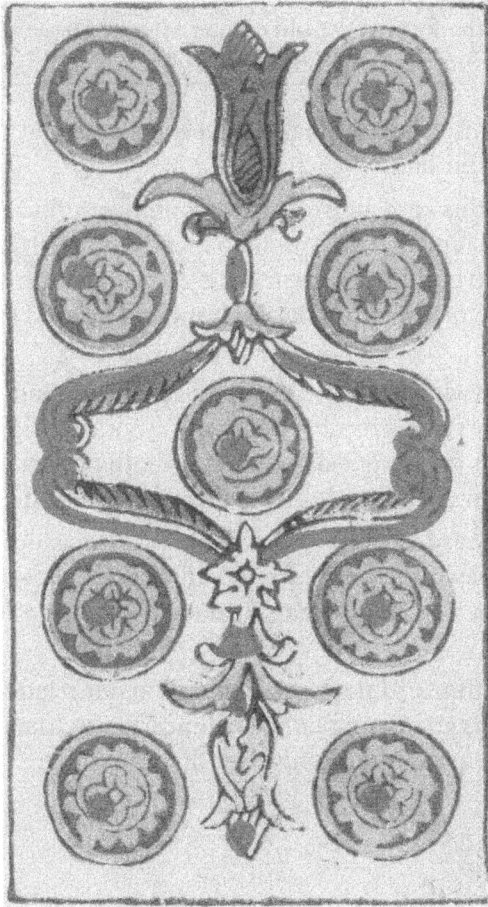

Ten of Coins

DIVINATORY MEANING
Family prosperity, success, material security. Family matters, buying a house or business, domains, inheritance.

INVERTED
Misfortune in the family, the old can be a heavy burden. Loss or problems with an inheritance. Money risk, robbery, gambling, dissipation.

The Ten of Coins is a card that suggests a stable and prosperous life within a close-knit family.

f we are alone, this card suggests the possibility of finding a stable and lasting relationship in which both partners support each other and work together to build a common life, but to achieve this goal, it would be advisable to expand our social environment beyond the scope of our family.

If we are already with someone, the Ten of Coins can indicate a relationship in which we enjoy great harmony and emotional stability, as well as material benefits and financial security for both parties. It is a solid and stable relationship in which both partners feel safe and cared for.

In general, this card suggests a flourishing relationship, which has the potential to prosper in the future. It can also indicate an engagement or marriage that will bring great satisfaction as well as emotional and financial stability.

If it is inverted, this card suggests problems in our relationships or family. Stability fades and is supplanted by uncertainty. The irresponsibility of others may cause our loss and bitter disappointment.

Page of Coins

DIVINATORY MEANING
Calm and studious, practical, educated, investigative, careful, kind, generous, thoughtful, introverted. Good administrator. Bearer of good news or messages related to money.

INVERTED
Irresponsible, wasteful, illogical, rebellious. Lack of purpose, unable to persevere in anything. Bad news. Loss of money

The Page of Coins is often seen as a messenger or bearer of news related to work, finances, and material success. In the context of love, it can represent a practical and pragmatic approach in relationships, where a couple seeks to build a solid and stable foundation for the future.

If we are alone, the Page of Coins suggests that this is a good time to focus on our goals and career, and that we may meet someone who shares our values and goals. It can also indicate that there is someone young and serious, but a little shy, who is interested in us.

If we are in a relationship, this card suggests that we should pay more attention to the financial and stability needs of our relationship. It can also indicate that it is a good time to invest time and effort in developing practical and financial skills that can help us create a stable and secure life for our family group.

In general, the Page of Coins is a card that encourages us to be practical and to seek stability and security in our love relationships. Like all pages, this card indicates news and messages, emphasizing that in any relationship, it is important to keep the channels of communication smooth.

If the Page of Coins is inverted, it may refer to someone who does not know how to handle money or organize his life, a rebel without a cause who does not know where he is going. This card warns us against people with these characteristics and recommends us to organize our lives in a more practical way.

Knight of Coins

DIVINATORY MEANING
Mature and responsible, methodical, practical, persevering, industrious, helpful and reliable. A trained administrator. Important matters related to money. He goes in search of fortune and knows how to defend it. Traveling salesman. Productive expression of creativity.

INVERTED
Unreliable. Lazy, narrow-minded, careless or clumsy, idle. Stagnation, unable to adapt. He pursues fortune without being able to obtain it.

The Knight of Coins represents a practical and stable approach in love relationships. This knight is loyal, hard-working and trustworthy, which makes him a good life partner for someone looking for a stable relationship.

If we are alone, this card can indicate that we are looking for a serious and committed relationship that has the possibility of leading to something lasting. The Knight of Coins can indicate the characteristic of a person with whom we are in contact or the type of relationship that would be suitable for us.

If we are already in a relationship, the Knight of Coins indicates a strong commitment and dedication to making the relationship work. It can mean that we are working hard to keep our relationship on a strong footing and that we are committed to doing whatever it takes to make it work for the long term.

In general, the Knight of Coins is a good omen for love and relationships, especially if we are looking for a serious and committed relationship. Of course, it all depends on the cards flanking it; by itself, the Knight of Coins is not a romantic personality, only if it is accompanied by one or more cards related to feelings (such as cups, in general), it would mean a sentimental relationship.

If it is inverted, this card symbolizes a person who is not trustworthy or capable, someone clumsy and careless. When it comes to interpersonal relationships, this lack of positive qualities does not bode well for them.

CAVALLIER·DE·DENIER:

Queen of Coins

DIVINATORY MEANING
Good, rich and charitable woman, with a big heart. Pragmatic, realistic, liberal and calm, but ambitious. Prosperity, security. Fortune through a woman. She is the Mother Earth, generous in gifts. Self-confidence, daring, certainty.

INVERTED
Presumptuous, negligent, fickle, foolish. Distrustful and insecure, fearful. Resistance to change, suspicion, hostility. She only cares about money.

The Queen of Coins is related to prosperity, material security and generosity. This card symbolizes a woman with the characteristics described in the divinatory meaning, someone with common sense, who knows her worth, but does not use her advantages to the detriment of others, but to help them. This person can be a great help to the seeker, if the neighboring cards confirm it.

If we are alone, this card indicates a generous and good woman, with whom, depending on the neighboring cards, we can establish a friendship or love relationship. The Queen of Coins can also indicate that a woman will support us in our projects.

If we are already in a relationship, the Queen of Coins indicates a practical and rational attitude, but also magnanimous, towards love relationships, and promises stability. The Queen of Coins is mature and responsible in her relationships, and she values honesty and loyalty in her partner.

In summary, the Queen of Coins emphasizes the importance of responsibility and the ability to share, in order to sustain satisfying and lasting relationships.

If is inverted, the Queen of Coins indicates an insecure person, who tries to present a grand façade to the world, and only knows how to receive, not give. She may not be a bad person, but she is not trustworthy and can easily turn against us.

REYNE·DE·DENIER·

King of Coins

DIVINATORY MEANING
Firm, phlegmatic, intelligent, capable in mathematics and finance, loyal and generous friend and/or husband. Prosperous trader, banker, experienced boss. Slow to anger, but relentless if unfairly provoked. Judicious investments, confidence and security, a prudent but optimistic vision. Pursuit of new achievements while keeping existing assets safe. Friendly with the consultant.

INVERTED
Corrupt, greedy, unfaithful, old and vicious, gambler, lender, speculator. Black magician. Dangerous if you enter in conflict with it. A bad manager, failed investment. Dissatisfaction with what you already have. A limited vision.

The King of Coins symbolizes a mature and successful man who has great financial acumen and a practical approach in life. When it comes to love, this card indicates that we are capable of committing ourselves to a stable and long-lasting relationship. The energy of the King of Coins suggests that our relationships will be based on trust, loyalty and mutual respect. This card also indicates that career and financial success can positively affect our love life and provide a solid foundation for a long-lasting and prosperous relationship.

If we are alone, the King of Coins indicates that we are extremely prudent and try to plan our lives in advance, to reduce risks. Possibly this is not the most appropriate way to approach love, which can benefit from a more flexible attitude, but it is our style. When this card refers to someone we know, the King of Coins indicates a man with the characteristics indicated in the divinatory meaning, who, depending on the neighboring cards, can be friendly, or with whom we can establish a relationship. He is someone trustworthy and calm, but if we betray him, he will be relentless with us.

If we are already in a relationship, the King of Coins can indicate that our relationship is based on stability and prudence, and that both partners work together to build a secure future. The King of Coins is not a card that promises great excitement, but it does guarantee stability and security.

ROY·DE·DENER·

In short, the King of Coins suggests searching for security and stability in romantic relationships, either by choosing a partner with these characteristics or, if we are already in a relationship, working together to build a stable and prosperous life.

If the King of Coins is inverted, it characterizes a dangerous man who should be avoided; if we don't bother him, he won't cause us problems, but it's not convenient to associate with him. As for a relationship, it is a bad omen, which portends dissatisfaction and mistakes.

Minor Arcana:
Swords

Ace of Swords

DIVINATORY MEANING
Conquest. Triumph achieved despite obstacles. Intense activity, firm and clear purpose. Pregnancy or childbirth. It is a card of excesses.

INVERTED
Excesses. Disaster or conquest followed by disaster, misuse of power, imbalance, confusion. Huge loss.

The Ace of Swords represents new beginnings, mental clarity, decision making, and action. Regarding love, this card can indicate that we are ready to make important decisions that will affect our relationship or to start a new relationship with mental clarity and determination. The Ace of Swords teaches us that clear and direct communication is necessary to advance our relationships.

If we are alone, the Ace of Swords suggests that we leave behind the negative emotions of the past and embrace a new beginning in love; let's cut with the old and dare to look for something new. If there are obstacles in our way, we can only overcome them with determination. Let's be bold in love.

If we are already in a relationship, the Ace of Swords can indicate a separation or a painful breakup, or perhaps an internal emotional conflict, which we must overcome to clarify a love relationship. We may need to make a difficult decision or face an unpleasant truth about our love situation. In some cases, it can also indicate a new beginning in love, but to be on the right track we need to express ourselves clearly and firmly. Another of the meanings of this card is pregnancy or childbirth (if other cards confirm it).

In general, the Ace of Swords suggests a confrontation, but also an opportunity to find truth and clarity in a relationship. This card also warns us against excesses, it is good to have clear goals and move forward boldly, but we must not abuse others; if we do, all our triumphs will be short-lived, because stable relationships cannot be maintained that way.

If the Ace of Swords is inverted, it indicates that we have not managed our social and/or love relationships well, and we will pay dearly for the abuses committed. Of course, if the neighboring cards link the Ace of Swords to another court card, these abuses may come from someone

else. In any case, inverted, the Ace of Swords suggests the end of a relationship.

Two of Swords

DIVINATORY MEANING
Equilibrium. Balanced forces, truce. Boundaries. Firmness, courage. Friendship, camaraderie. The will is forged in the fight.

INVERTED
Discord. Lack of control. Betrayal, lies, disloyalty, false friends.

The Two of Swords represents the antagonism of two opposing forces, a relationship where both parties respect each other and maintain a dynamic balance.

If we are alone, this card may indicate that we will have more chances of having new friends than new loves. There is a clear limit between friendship and love, which is not always possible to cross, and this card tells us that we must be clear about the limits to avoid possible conflicts.

If we are already in a relationship, the Two of Swords can indicate tensions and antagonisms in our relationship, but with clear communication and honesty, we will be able to overcome or handle them. Also this card can suggest that we will have to make an important decision and that we must choose between two options. It can also indicate a need for balance and harmony in our love relationships. It is advisable that we do not make hasty decisions, but allow ourselves time to reflect and carefully consider our options before making a decision.

In short, the Two of Swords reminds us to be honest with ourselves and with others about our feelings, and tells us that we need to know how to maintain balance in our relationships by setting clear boundaries.

When inverted, the Two of Swords indicates that the balance has been broken and that one partner in a relationship will cheat or betray the other one. This card advises us to be cautious and keep our guard up against lies and false loves and friends.

Three of Swords

DIVINATORY MEANING
Grief, tears, melancholy, separation, divorce, contention, conflict, postponement, absence. For a woman: the flight of her lover.

INVERTED
It has a similar meaning, but toned down: confusion, mistake, alienation, separation. A nun.

The Three of Swords is a card that reflects pain and grief. In love, it can represent a painful separation or a betrayal that causes great suffering. It can indicate a period of mourning, sadness, and emotional pain after a breakup or heartbreak.

If we are alone, the Three of Swords teaches us that as long as we do not leave behind the sorrows and longing for the people who are already in the past, we will not be able to move forward or establish good relationships with other people. It can also indicate a present, problematic and conflictive relationship; if we cannot solve the conflicts that pain us, it is better to terminate any joyless relationship.

If we are already in a relationship, the Three of Swords suggests miscommunication or a situation where two people are not on the same page emotionally and cannot find a way to reconcile. This card can indicate a temporary separation or conflict, infidelity, or even divorce, depending on the neighboring cards.

In general, the Three of Swords is a card that suggests that we need time to heal and recover before we can move forward in a new relationship. If we are already in a relationship, it indicates a lot of conflicts; we must decide if it is possible to save our relationship or if it is better to abandon it.

When inverted, this card's meanings are similar, but toned down. It is still a bad card for love, but more than great conflicts, it indicates confusion and disagreements, temporary estrangement, loneliness.

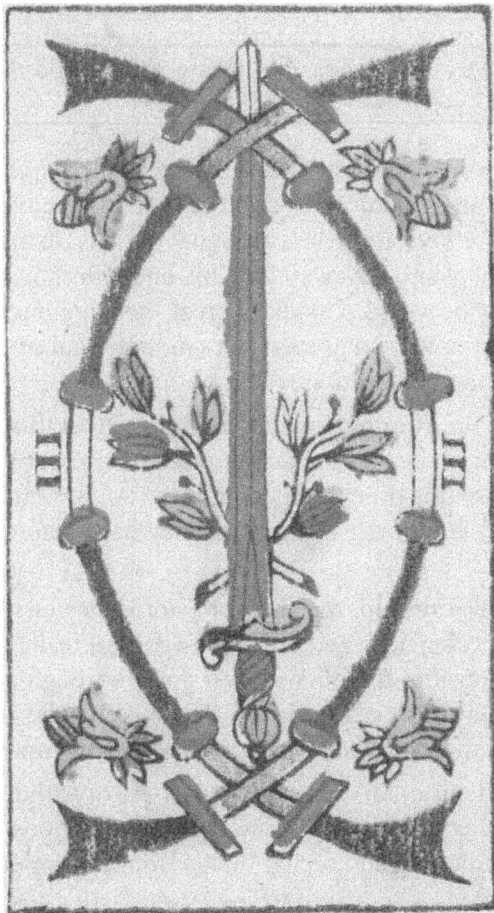

Four of Swords

DIVINATORY MEANING
Truce, loneliness, stagnation, restriction. Recovery of health after an illness, may indicate hospitalization. Spiritual retreat, meditation. Exile.

INVERTED
Renewed activity. Prudence, discretion and economy are recommended.

The Four of Swords suggests that we need to take time to reflect and meditate, and can symbolize a period of rest and recovery after a difficult time. As for love, this card can signal the need to make a truce in a conflicted relationship, get away for a bit, and reflect on what we really want to do. May be we need to take a break from arguments or conflicts in a relationship so we can process our emotions and come back with a clearer and calmer perspective.

If we are alone, the Four of Swords can indicate that this is a good time to pause our social life and focus on ourselves and our spiritual development. Let's use this time to reflect on what we want in a relationship and to heal any emotional wounds we may have before looking for a new love.

If we are in a relationship, the Four of Swords suggests that it may be helpful to take a step back and reflect on what we really want and need from the relationship. If we have been going through a difficult time with our partner, this card indicates that this may be a good time to take some time to recover our balance before trying to work things out.

In general, the Four of Swords indicates a time of withdrawal and solitude, when we temporarily withdraw from our relationships and try to calm down, meditating and seeing things from a new perspective.

When this card is inverted, it indicates that we will gradually overcome the secluded state in which we find ourselves and open up to social relationships and love again, but it advises us to do it little by little, step by step.

Five of Swords

DIVINATORY MEANING
Dispossession, defeat, crisis, humiliation, dishonor, degradation, demotion, loss, impotence, slander. It only remains to accept the inevitable. Alternatively, giving something up to avoid a conflict that cannot be won.

INVERTED
Anguish, uncertain future, danger of loss or defeat, warning against pride and betrayal. Funeral, bereavement, misfortune of a friend. Weakness, seduction.

The Five of Swords can be a difficult card when it comes to love and relationships. This card often represents deceit, betrayal, and dishonesty in relationships. It can indicate a situation where one person is manipulating another or using unethical tactics to gain power or control. This is not a good time for love.

If we are alone, the Five of Swords is a warning, the time is not conducive to taking risks in love or in social relationships. Let's not assume that the people we associate with are benign, we could be betrayed by a wolf in sheep's clothing. Let's be prudent and don't be fooled, if something is too good, it may not be what it seems.

If we are already in a relationship, the Five of Swords suggests that someone in the relationship is being dishonest or unreliable. It could also mean that we are being manipulated or used by another person. If we are facing a conflictive divorce, this card tells us to reach an agreement, even if it is not the best possible, before resorting to justice.

In general, this card tells us that it is important to pay attention to any unclear situation. Also, the Five of Swords may indicate that it is time for us to be more assertive and know how to protect ourselves from people who try to take advantage of us in love.

If this card is inverted, its meaning is less ominous, but it is still a warning against possible risks in the future, which may affect us or a friend. It also advises us against pride and betrayal, let us not be manipulated or seduced.

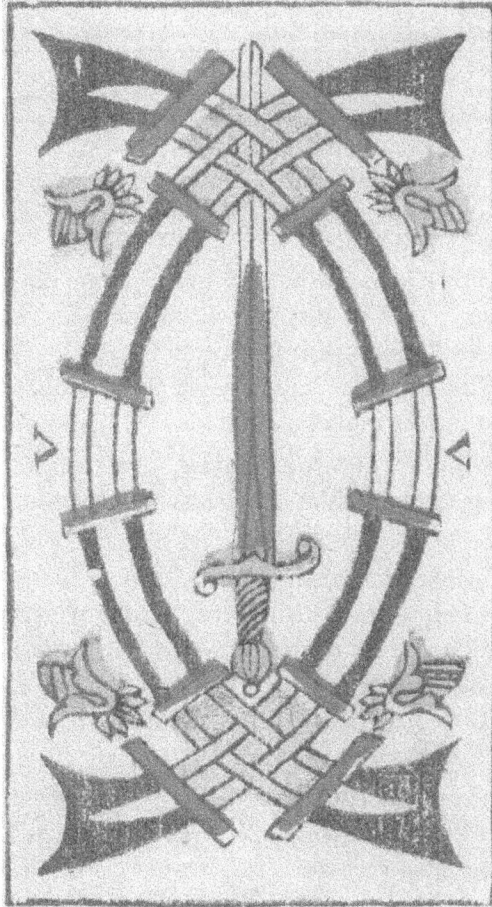

Six of Swords

DIVINATORY MEANING
Progress, overcoming difficulties, change of scenery. Travel by water to a new home, and/or travel on the plane of consciousness. Smart effort, deserved success, inspiration, study, science.

INVERTED
Stagnation, impediment to travel, difficulties cannot be overcome, lack of inspiration. Unfavorable outcome or judgment. Confession, declaration.

The Six of Swords shows us the way to overcome our limitations and conflicts in love, which in this case is moving forward, looking for new opportunities, growing spiritually, and leaving behind everything that limits us. This card can also indicate emigration, or to relocate to another place to pursue higher studies.

If we are alone, the Six of Swords advises us to renew ourselves, seek new horizons and new relationships, leaving behind our old circle of friends.

If we are already in a relationship, the Six of Swords can indicate a moment of transition in a relationship, that we are overcoming a difficult or painful situation and are moving towards a more promising future. It also teaches us that we must grow spiritually in order to overcome difficulties in our love life. If other cards confirm this, it can also indicate that we will leave our home.

In general, the Six of Swords is a card of hope and progress. It indicates that although the road ahead seems difficult, there is light at the end of the tunnel and change is possible, if we are willing to broaden our horizons.

If it is inverted, this card indicates that we are blocked and do not know how to surmount our problems; we keep repeating behavior models that don't benefit us and we are incapable of innovating; perhaps we are stuck in a relationship that doesn't not benefit us. We will not be able to overcome our problems with other people until we grow spiritually.

Seven of Swords

DIVINATORY MEANING
Risky attempt, perhaps to appropriate what belongs to others or to spy, with partial or unpredictable results. Hope, longing, desire. Better skill than strength. Journey, escape. Illicit love affair.

INVERTED
Difficulty making a decision, indecision. Good advice, warning, better think twice before acting. Arguments, complaints, disappointment in the family or with a friend.

The Seven of Swords suggests that we are trying to achieve something that would normally be out of our reach, perhaps it is a relationship with someone who is already committed, or with someone above our social circle. Since it is not possible to achieve our wishes openly, we try to achieve them using skill rather than force. Let's keep in mind that one of the meanings of this card is illicit love affair.

If we are alone, the Seven of Swords suggests that we are looking for a love affair, rather than a stable relationship; we may succeed, but it is very possible that things will not end as well as we hope. Likewise, the Seven of Swords can be a sign that we should be careful with those who are not what they seem and who may not be trustworthy.

If we are already in a relationship, the Seven of Swords suggests the possibility of deceit, betrayal or dishonesty. Perhaps the weaker party in the relationship uses subterfuges to gain advantage. There may be secrets or hidden information that threatens the trust and stability of the relationship, and it is possible that it will come to light. It's important to watch for any signs of cheating or suspicious behavior and address it openly and honestly with our partner. This can also be a good time to reflect on our own behavior, that may be contributing to a lack of trust or communication with our partner.

In general the Seven of Swords suggests that things are unclear and nothing is what it seems to be; it is possible that — blinded by passion — we get into trouble. If we have a conflict with someone, it is better to come to an amicable settlement instead of looking for a confrontation.

When the Seven of Swords appears inverted, it indicates a conflict with someone close to us. If we're not sure what to do to overcome the conflict, we'd better seek advice, not rush into action.

Eight of Swords

Divinatory Meaning
Interference, captivity, restriction, self-limitation, paralyzing indecision, imbalance, confusion. Crisis or temporary illness. Betrayal, slander, censorship. Bewitchment.

Inverted
New beginning, new options. Freedom from the bonds of the past or from enemies. Seeing things with a new perspective.

The Eight of Swords suggests lack of clarity, which paralyzes us and prevents us from making a decision or moving forward. In the context of love, it can indicate that we feel trapped in a relationship or situation that makes us unhappy and we don't see a way out.

If we are alone, this card can suggest that we are trapped by our own beliefs or thought patterns about love, which prevent us from moving forward and finding a satisfying relationship. It can be a reminder to review our expectations and allow ourselves to experience new things in our search for love. It is also possible that someone is deceiving us.

If we are in a relationship, the Eight of Swords indicates confusion and the inability to get out of the emotional quagmire in which we find ourselves. Our partner may be cheating on us, fueling our confusion to manipulate us to their liking, but it is also possible that our own insecurity is holding us back and preventing us from moving forward, as if we were clinging to the relationship out of obligation or fear of being alone. As usual, the neighboring cards will allow us to determine what is the cause of our problems.

In general, the Eight of Swords indicates an intellectual and emotional blockage, a period in which we do not see things clearly. The only way to overcome this blockage is to remove the blindfold and see reality clearly, overcoming our prejudices and not letting ourselves be influenced by what other people tell us.

If this card is inverted, it is a good omen, it indicates that we will overcome the confusing period that kept us tied to the past — and to the machinations of other people — and we will see things clearly. That is the first step to recover our freedom of thought and action.

Nine of Swords

DIVINATORY MEANING
Suffering, despair, illness, depression, martyrdom. A heavy burden. Cloistered, a priest. Obsessive worry. It can indicate the death of a loved one. Malice, cruelty, magical attack. Spontaneous abortion.

INVERTED
Beginning of a recovery. Time heals everything. Resignation; accept the inevitable, stop worrying, stop thinking about it, let go. Hope and charity.

The Nine of Swords is often associated with anxiety, depression, and fear. This card can indicate that we are experiencing great fear or concern related to our current relationship or love situation.

If we are alone, the Nine of Swords can indicate that we are afraid of making a commitment or starting a new relationship due to past traumas or disappointments. We may isolate ourselves so as not to take any risk, but those who risk nothing gain nothing.

If we are in a relationship, this card can indicate that we are afraid that something will go wrong or that our partner will abandon us. The Nine of Swords can also indicate that we are very stressed in our love relationship. We may be worried about something that has happened or what might happen in the future, preventing us from fully enjoying our relationship. Likewise (but only if other cards confirm it) this card can indicate a loss, it can refer to the death of a loved one or to a pregnancy that does not reach term.

In general, the Nine of Swords is a card that indicates depression, worry, and anxiety. If we are experiencing these feelings, it is important that we talk to our partner or seek help to overcome them and improve our relationship life.

If it is inverted, the Nine of Swords indicates that we will overcome the fears and bitterness that made us unhappy. It teaches us to look ahead and accept past losses with equanimity; we will never forget what has happened, but we cannot and should not let those bad memories cloud our present and our future.

Ten of Swords

DIVINATORY MEANING
Great misfortune, ruin of plans and relationships, desolation, the end of an illusion, defeat, loss, short illness. This card represents the nadir, the lowest point of this cycle of fortune; from now on things can only get better. It does not indicate death or violence.

INVERTED
Improvement, relief. Something of profit or success. Will to overcome problems.

The Ten of Swords usually portends bad news, as it represents the end of something. It can indicate a breakup, betrayal or a painful situation in a relationship. It can also mean emotional loss or bereavement. However, it is important to remember that in the Tarot, no card is completely good or bad on its own, but must be interpreted in the context of the question and the cards that surround it. In some cases, the Ten of Swords can indicate the need to let go of a relationship that is no longer healthy or happy in order to move on and find something better.

If we are alone, this card indicates that our hopes will not be fulfilled and our relationships will not prosper. If we have an ongoing project, it will fail. The best thing we can do is not lose confidence in ourselves and wait until the situation improves, seeing how, even if only in small ways, we can improve the situation.

If we are currently in a relationship, the Ten of Swords is a bad omen, since this card is associated with pain and loss, and in the context of love, it can be a sign of a breakup or the sad end of a relationship. However, it can also indicate that it is time to let go of what no longer serves us and move on, and that it is important to look to the future instead of clinging to the past.

In general, the Ten of Swords teaches us that everything is transitory, and we must learn to be in the flow, and adapt to what life brings us, good and bad. In any case, this card indicates temporary misfortune, but it is always up to us to improve our lives and cultivate good relationships that make us happy. Also, sometimes the Ten of Swords can be a sign that we need time to heal and to be ready for a new relationship in

the future. This card also teaches us that the best way to heal our emotional wounds is to help others.

When it is inverted, the Ten of Swords promises us an improvement in our situation. It will be something gradual, but with perseverance, we will be able to overcome the bad moment.

Page of Swords

Divinatory Meaning
Logical and penetrating, aggressive, tough, alert. Agile of mind and body. Espionage, messages, diplomacy, prudence, practical wisdom. Supervisor, administrator; watchman, investigator, bodyguard. Planning for the future, looking for the best option.

Inverted
Malicious, conniving, treacherous, vindictive, meddler, indiscreet. Night prowler. Unexpected news or disturbance, impotence. Health problems.

The Page of Swords is associated with intellectuality, logic, and clear and concise communication. In love, it can indicate that we are taking a very rational and cold attitude with our partner, placing too much emphasis on logical thinking and neglecting emotions and feelings. This card can also indicate that we are dealing with a person who is very analytical and critical in love, and it can be difficult to connect emotionally with such a character.

If we are alone, the Page of Swords teaches us that, in love, it is important to try to find a balance between reason and emotion, and pay attention to the feelings and needs of both members of a love relationship. May be we are very demanding and are looking for the perfect partner, perhaps it would be good to relax a bit and live a little more in the present, without worrying so much about the future. Likewise, this card could indicate the appearance of a person with the characteristics of the Page of Swords in our life, someone who is very intellectual and who values truth and honesty above all else.

If we are already in a relationship, the Page of Swords can indicate that this is a good time to look at our relationship objectively and assess whether our needs and those of our partner are being met. It can also be a time to try to improve communication with our partner, to make sure that we are understanding each other well.

In general, the Page of Swords is a card that focuses on the mind and communication, which suggests that our success in love will depend to a large extent on our ability to communicate with and understand our partner. This card also urges us to keep our guard up and not gleefully

accept everything we are told; a little skepticism will avoid disappointment in the future.

When the Page of Swords is inverted it is a bad omen in love; it is possible that someone is acting against us, even if he pretends to be our friend or swears love to us. It is advisable to act prudently, do not trust anyone blindly.

Knight of Swords

DIVINATORY MEANING
Brave, active, intelligent, subtle, versatile, changeable, very skilful and prepared, dominant, with good intentions. The image of the knight-errant, dedicated and persevering. Energy and means to advance. The arrival or departure of misfortune. Military, detective, investigator.

INVERTED
Ruthless, fanatic, extravagant, tyrannical and destructive. War. A dangerous fool. Scam, deceit.

The Knight of Swords describes someone impetuous and with good intentions, with an honest and direct character. Like all the knights of the Tarot, this card indicates arrivals and departures, in this case it can indicate the arrival or departure of love.

If we are alone, the Knight of Swords can symbolize someone who will appear in our life, or perhaps it represents the way in which we relate to others. In love, this card suggests that we can be a bit domineering and perhaps too intense in the expression of our feelings; even if no one questions our honesty, we could benefit from learning to temper our behavior a bit and embellish our words with a bit of courtesy and poetry. This card also suggests that we are looking for someone who is very intelligent and rational, but perhaps we need to be more open to our emotions to achieve a deep emotional connection.

If we are already in a relationship, the Knight of Swords suggests that perhaps we are being too critical of ourselves or our partner, or that we are too demanding, which can negatively affect the relationship. It is important to remember that love also has an emotional component and that compassion and empathy can be just as important as logic and reason. This card also may indicate the coming or going of love, that is, somebody new may appear, or somebody may leave (if other cards suggest it).

When this card is inverted, this can mean separation or divorce. The Knight of Swords indicates an extreme and destructive conflict with a fanatic, someone irrational and very destructive; let's be careful and stay away from people with these characteristics.

CAVALLIER·DE·SPEE·

Queen of Swords

DIVINATORY MEANING
Elegant but strict. Agile of mind and body, fair, individualistic, tough. It can be a dancer, a widow or a woman without children. This card also means deprivation, absence, separation, mourning. Defense of the territory. Intelligence, lucidity.

INVERTED
Paranoid, cruel, malicious, deceitful, devious, slanderous, jealous, narrow-minded schemer. Prejudiced, unable to adapt to the new. A malicious woman is our enemy and she can harm us.

The Queen of Swords is a figure that represents intelligence, cunning and independence. When it comes to love, her presence can signify the need to make difficult decisions in a relationship, to be honest and upfront about how we feel, and to set healthy boundaries to protect ourselves.

If we are alone, the Queen of Swords indicates that we may be at a time in our life where we are very focused on our career or our personal goals, which can make it a bit difficult to find a loving relationship. It may also be that we are taking time to heal from a loss and need time for ourselves before getting involved in a new relationship. In the event that this card represents someone who comes into contact with us, it would indicate a widow or a mature woman without children.

If we are already in a relationship, the Queen of Swords can refer to a person who comes into our life, or describe how our relationship works. In the realm of love, this card suggests a lucid and unromantic attitude towards our partner, where we value honesty and sincerity above all else, even if it means facing painful truths. The Queen of Swords represents a very strong mental energy, and in love it can indicate that we are more focused on the practical and rational aspects of our relationship than on emotions and feelings. It can be a sign that we need to find the right balance between our head and our heart in order to achieve a more fulfilling relationship.

In general, this card is not very conducive to relationships, since it rather indicates absence, distance and mourning, but it still teaches us that in all our relationships we must balance our feelings well with our ra-

·REJNE · DE·SPEE·

tionality. The Queen of Swords also indicates equanimity, balance and grace and while these qualities are not very romantic, they will allow our relationships to last a long time.

If this card is inverted, it is a warning against someone malicious, possibly a slanderous and jealous woman, who wants to harm us. It is also a wake-up call so that we ourselves are not narrow-minded or jealous.

King of Swords

Divinatory Meaning
A man with authority. Active, logical, intelligent, full of ideas, expert. Courageous, firm in friendship and enmity, intelligent, self-controlled, modern, daring. Magistrate, man of laws, prosecutor. Surgeon, chief, military, widower, professional. Powerful ally or a good advisor. A judgment.

Inverted
It represents authority, power placed at the service of malevolence, an evil man who seeks to do harm. Obstinate, cruel, suspicious. Formidable enemy. Conflict.

The King of Swords generally represents a mature and experienced man who is very logical, analytical and objective in his thoughts and actions. He can be an excellent friend, but also a fearsome enemy. Like the Queen of Swords, this card suggests the need to balance the head and heart in our relationships.

If we are alone, the King of Swords can suggest that we are determined to put the past behind us and face the future, even though our heart still yearns for the past. It also indicates that we will be bold in love, but we will not abandon ourselves to it, since we will try to keep our desires and passions under control. In the event that the card refers to another person, he would be someone with the characteristics already described.

If we are already in a relationship, this card suggests that it is more of a relationship of convenience than one based on passion. The King of Swords does not share power, so in any relationship, only one of the members will have command. Another possible meaning is a divorce trial.

In general, the symbology of the King of Swords is not the best for romantic relationships, although it indicates order, justice and regularity, so balanced and mutually beneficial relationships are possible.

If this card is inverted, the King of Swords becomes an enemy as formidable as it is ruthless; this card is an omen of conflict.

· R·O·Y · DE·SPEE ·

www.ingramcontent.com/pod-product-compliance
Lightning Source LLC
Chambersburg PA
CBHW051422090426
42737CB00014B/2783